Sound Teaching

Sound Teaching explores the ways in which music psychology and education can meet to inspire developments in the teaching and learning of music performance.

The book is based on music practitioners' research into aspects of their own professional practice. Each chapter addresses a specific topic related to musical communication and expression, performance confidence and enjoyment, or skill development in individual and group learning. It explains the background of the research, outlines main findings, and provides suggestions for practical applications. *Sound Teaching* provides a research-informed approach to teaching and contributes to music tutors' professional development in teaching children and adults of various ages and abilities.

Sound Teaching is written for vocal and instrumental music teachers, music performers with a portfolio career, and music students at conservatoires and universities. Music students undertaking practice-related research will find examples of research methodologies and projects that are informative for their studies. Musical participants of all kinds – students, teachers, performers, and audiences – will find new ways of understanding their practice and experience through research.

Henrique Meissner is Honorary Research Fellow at The University of Sheffield and Course Leader for Practice-based Research in the Master of Music at the Prins Claus Conservatorium in Groningen.

Renee Timmers is Professor of Psychology of Music at The University of Sheffield.

Stephanie E. Pitts is Professor of Music Education at The University of Sheffield.

Sound Teaching
A Research-Informed Approach to Inspiring Confidence, Skill, and Enjoyment in Music Performance

Edited by
Henrique Meissner,
Renee Timmers, and
Stephanie E. Pitts

LONDON AND NEW YORK

First published 2022
by Routledge
2 Park Square, Milton Park, Abingdon, Oxon OX14 4RN

and by Routledge
605 Third Avenue, New York, NY 10158

Routledge is an imprint of the Taylor & Francis Group, an informa business

© 2022 selection and editorial matter, Henrique Meissner, Renee Timmers, Stephanie E. Pitts; individual chapters, the contributors

The right of Henrique Meissner, Renee Timmers, Stephanie E. Pitts to be identified as the authors of the editorial material, and of the authors for their individual chapters, has been asserted in accordance with sections 77 and 78 of the Copyright, Designs and Patents Act 1988.

All rights reserved. No part of this book may be reprinted or reproduced or utilised in any form or by any electronic, mechanical, or other means, now known or hereafter invented, including photocopying and recording, or in any information storage or retrieval system, without permission in writing from the publishers.

Trademark notice: Product or corporate names may be trademarks or registered trademarks, and are used only for identification and explanation without intent to infringe.

British Library Cataloguing-in-Publication Data
A catalogue record for this book is available from the British Library

Library of Congress Cataloging-in-Publication Data
A catalog record has been requested for this book

ISBN: 978-0-367-62213-8 (hbk)
ISBN: 978-0-367-62217-6 (pbk)
ISBN: 978-1-003-10838-2 (ebk)

DOI: 10.4324/9781003108382

Typeset in NewBaskerville
by Apex CoVantage, LLC

Contents

List of figures	vii
Note on editors	viii
List of contributors	ix
Acknowledgements	xi
List of transcription symbols	xii

1 Introduction: a research-informed approach to vocal and instrumental music learning and teaching   1
HENRIQUE MEISSNER, RENEE TIMMERS, AND STEPHANIE E. PITTS

PART I
Musicians as teachers   11

2 How musical learning experiences have an impact on music educators' attitudes and practices   13
CLÁUDIA BRAZ NUNES

3 Traditional musicians as teachers: sharing skills for participation   24
JOSEPHINE L. MILLER

PART II
Developing specialist musical skills   35

4 Teaching children and teenagers expressive music performance   37
HENRIQUE MEISSNER

5	Developing timbre on the piano: interactions between sound, body, and concepts SHEN LI	48
6	Mobilising improvisation skills in classically trained musicians JONATHAN AYERST	61

PART III
Group leadership and interaction in ensembles   73

7	Communication and interaction in ensemble rehearsal NICOLA PENNILL	75
8	Conductors as teachers: the effects of verbal feedback on singers' confidence, enjoyment, and performance quality MICHAEL BONSHOR	87

PART IV
Strategies for enhancing musical confidence and enjoyment   99

9	Singing and signing with Deaf and hearing impaired young people GAIL DUDSON	101
10	Teaching pre-performance routines to improve students' performance experience MARY HAWKES	111
11	The teacher's role in the enhancement of students' performance experience ELSA PERDOMO-GUEVARA	122
12	Reflections on implications for sound teaching, lifelong music learning, and future research HENRIQUE MEISSNER, RENEE TIMMERS, AND STEPHANIE E. PITTS	132

Index   141

Figures

2.1	Layers of interaction affecting educators' attitudes toward music education	16
3.1	Transcription of an extract from the tune 'Spootiskerry'	29
4.1	'Toolkit' of strategies for teaching expressive music performance	44
5.1	The perception of piano timbre to be tense for performances performed under the instruction of 'tense' or 'relaxed'. Performances were presented as audio-only, audio-video, or video-only	51
5.2	Hand-gestures illustrating timbral intentions	56
6.1	Graphic design for an improvised Prelude and Fugue	65
6.2	The opening bars of the third movement of Trio Sonata BWV 525 for organ, by J. S. Bach (1685–1750), over my own harmonic and rhythmic reductions which functioned as templates for improvisation	66
7.1	A dynamic model of performance preparation	79
7.2	Key events in performance preparation as experienced by group members in relation to three phases of development: exploration, transition (grey shaded area), and integration	82
9.1	Pippa's illustration of her favourite song	108

Note on editors

Henrique Meissner is Honorary Research Fellow at The University of Sheffield and Course Leader for Practice-based Research in the Master of Music at the Prins Claus Conservatorium in Groningen. Henrique studied recorder at the Utrecht Conservatoire and has extensive experience as an instrumental tutor. She obtained her MA and PhD in Music Psychology in Education at The University of Sheffield. Her research interests are related to instrumental learning and teaching, performance expression, and young musicians' development.

Renee Timmers is Professor of Psychology of Music at The University of Sheffield. She was educated in the Netherlands, where she obtained an MA in Musicology and PhD in Psychology. Her work includes publications on expressive performance of music, expression and perception of emotion in music, interactions between cognition and emotion in music, and cross-modal experiences of music. She is co-editor of the volumes *Expressiveness in music performance: Empirical approaches across styles and cultures* (OUP, 2014) and *The Routledge companion to music cognition* (Routledge, 2017). She directs the research centre Music Mind Machine in Sheffield and is acting President of the European Society for the Cognitive Sciences of Music (ESCOM 2019–2021).

Stephanie E. Pitts is Professor of Music Education at The University of Sheffield, with research interests in musical participation, arts audiences, and lifelong learning. She is the author of books including *Valuing musical participation* (Ashgate, 2005), *Chances and choices: Exploring the impact of music education* (OUP, 2012), *Music and mind in everyday life* (Clarke, Dibben & Pitts, OUP, 2010), *Understanding audience engagement in the contemporary arts* (Pitts & Price, Routledge, 2021), and a co-edited volume on audience experience, *Coughing and clapping* (Burland & Pitts, Ashgate, 2014). She is Director of the Sheffield Performer and Audience Research Centre.

Contributors

Jonathan Ayerst is a professional organist, pianist, and choral conductor. He works with the contemporary music ensemble Remix Ensemble of Porto, Portugal. Jonathan was awarded the Charles Alan Bryars Organ Scholarship by The University of Sheffield for his PhD project on learning techniques for classical improvisation.

Michael Bonshor is Course Director for the MA Music Psychology in Education, Performance and Wellbeing at The University of Sheffield, a researcher co-investigator with the University of Derby, and the author of *The confident choir: A handbook for leaders of group singing* (Rowman & Littlefield, 2017).

Cláudia Braz Nunes studied Music Education and Choral Conducting at the Lisbon Music University and obtained her MA and PhD at The University of Sheffield. She is involved with music outreach activities at the Royal Academy of Music. Her research interests focus on lifelong engagement with music.

Gail Dudson is the director of Yorkshire Youth & Music, a charity working with children in challenging circumstances across Yorkshire. During her Master's study at The University of Sheffield, Gail investigated the musical and social benefits of music making for Deaf and hearing impaired young people.

Mary Hawkes is a piano teacher and researcher. She has worked as a qualified tennis coach, primary school teacher, and music therapist. She obtained her MA and PhD from The University of Sheffield. Her interest is connecting music and sport in research and practice.

Shen Li is a post-doc researcher at the Department of Psychology, Central China Normal University in Wuhan. Her research background is in piano performance (BA) and psychology of music (MA, MMus, PhD). Her research interests focus on the conceptualisation of piano timbre and musical behaviour in cyberspace.

Josephine L. Miller is an ethnomusicologist and community musician based in Scotland. She holds a PhD from The University of Sheffield, and in 2017 received the Hamish Henderson Award for Services to Traditional Music. She is the author of *A pedagogy of participation: Community-based traditional music in Scotland* (Routledge).

Nicola Pennill is a post-doctoral researcher at the Royal Northern College of Music and Honorary Research Fellow at The University of Sheffield, where she also obtained her PhD. With a background as a musician and in management consulting, her interest in ensembles is rooted in group dynamics.

Elsa Perdomo-Guevara is Honorary Research Fellow at The University of Sheffield. She trained as a pianist at the Conservatoire National Supérieur de Musique de Paris and taught at conservatoires in France and Brazil. She is particularly interested in helping institutions to promote musicians' wellbeing.

Acknowledgements

The ideas for this book arose from the Sound Teaching workshops in October 2018 realised with support from Widening Participation, Faculty of Arts & Humanities, The University of Sheffield. Research reported in the book was supported by PhD scholarships from Arts and Humanities Research Council, Research Councils UK (HM), Charles Allan Bryars (JA), Chinese Scholarship Council (SL), Faculty of Arts and Humanities, The University of Sheffield (MH), White Rose College of Arts and Humanities (NP), funding from SEMPRE (HM), and MA funding from Yorkshire Youth and Music (GD). In addition to Stephanie E. Pitts and Renee Timmers, supervisors for the doctoral projects featured in the book included Nicola Dibben, Dermot Breslin, Dorothy Ker, Catherine Laws, and Victoria Rowe. We are indebted by the invaluable contribution of participants in the research, the feedback and input received from participants at the Sound Teaching workshops, and the continued support in event organisation and research pursuit through our Sheffield Performer and Audience Research Centre (*sparc.dept.shef.ac.uk*) and Music, Mind, Machine research centre (*mmm.sites.sheffield.ac.uk*). Readers who would like to respond to the book are invited to get in touch with us through our personal or research centre webpages.

Transcription symbols

[text] Is used to clarify what the transcriber thought that the speaker meant or if the transcriber added a word.
(text) Is used for utterances that were difficult to understand. The brackets indicate that this is the most likely possibility of what the speaker said.
[. . .] Indicates that the authors have left something out, usually because it is impossible to hear what is being said, or because it was too long to cite.
((text)) Double parentheses contain a description of events.
Text in *italics* denotes emphasis by the speaker.

1 Introduction

A research-informed approach to vocal and instrumental music learning and teaching

Henrique Meissner, Renee Timmers, and Stephanie E. Pitts

Sound Teaching is a celebration of what can happen when music education practitioners, musicians, and researchers have the opportunity to talk to one another. Ideas are shared, connections are forged, assumptions are challenged, and everyone leaves the exchange with food for thought. This should not be a rarity, but the practicalities of life as an instrumental teacher, a student, or a university lecturer all too often mean that we pursue our immediate demands and pressing deadlines without taking time to pause, think, and discuss.

This book took shape during 2020, when the pandemic lockdowns caused us as editors to miss our regular face-to-face interactions with colleagues, and the stimulus of incidental conversations that create a shared sense of academic, educational, or musical purpose. This was another reminder to us that many of our contributors know all too well the challenges of working in isolation: instrumental teachers often lack opportunities to exchange pedagogical and professional views with like-minded colleagues, and doctoral students crave the intellectual exchange of connections with others working on similar topics.

We believe that fostering communication between musicians and researchers can benefit music performance and teaching practices, as well as research in music psychology and music education. Traditionally, a lot of learning and teaching in European classical and folk music is based on practitioners' experience; tutors develop their pedagogy on what they feel works well, and what has worked for them in the past (e.g., Mills & Smith, 2003). Although pedagogical practices evolve over time, it can be fruitful to deliberately explore new ways of teaching and investigate strategies based on systematic research

DOI: 10.4324/9781003108382-1

and empirical evidence. In addition, collaboration with teachers and performers helps researchers to continue developing and refining research questions and directions. Thus, research can inform music education and performance practice and vice versa.

Indeed, the topics and questions that are explored in the chapters of this book arose out of the authors' teaching, performing, or conducting practice: for instance, Cláudia Braz Nunes's reflections on her everyday decisions as a classroom music teacher led her to examine music educators' attitudes to teaching (Chapter 2); Jonathan Ayerst's wish to improvise in classical genres motivated him to investigate learning improvisation skills systematically (Chapter 6); Mary Hawkes and Elsa Perdomo-Guevara's experiences with performance anxiety inspired them to explore ways for enhancing their students' confidence and joy in performance (Chapters 10 and 11). Each chapter originated from questions embedded in daily teaching or performing practice, and many chapters contain honest descriptions of the starting points of the authors. Thus, the book provides examples of practitioner research that could contribute to the professional development of vocal and instrumental music teachers.

Aims of the book

The main aim of this book is to show how a research-informed approach can help develop vocal and instrumental music learning and performing. The chapters address topics that are central to music education practices including musicians as teachers, the development of specialist musical skills, musical communication and expression, and performance confidence and enjoyment. By sharing our findings and explaining our own motivations and the research methods that we used, we hope to develop greater understanding of the ways in which research can inform practice, and to receive feedback from practitioners so that this can inform future research. Growing understanding of the teaching and learning process and of communication in lessons and ensembles can help to enhance the music participation of all involved: students, teachers, performers, and audience. Feedback from our own students and the responses of music education professionals who attended the *Sound Teaching* (2018, 2019) conferences where initial versions of most of these chapters were presented, showed that there is an appetite for recent, practical research on effective musical learning and development in accessible language.

What is music psychology research and how is it relevant?

The development of expert performance of music tends to be surrounded by mystery, as most of the required practice, rehearsal, and teaching happens behind closed doors. In studies in the field of music psychology, processes of learning and practice related to music performance take centre stage. These studies aim to develop greater understanding of, and as such demystify, what is happening in musical learning and performance. Music psychology research has developed rapidly in recent decades (for introductory review chapters, see e.g., Ashley & Timmers, 2017), generating enhanced insight into processes of learning, expression, and emotion[1] related to music education and performance, providing opportunities for the professional development of instrumental teachers[2] and portfolio musicians, and addressing debates about the purpose and impact of music education (see e.g., Pitts, 2017). The application of music psychology findings to music education practice can facilitate sound music teaching.

In our title, we have placed the emphasis on *Sound Teaching*, but the perspective of the learner is obviously strongly embedded in any consideration of effective teaching. When the characteristics and needs of the learner are at the heart of music education, learning can thrive. Teaching and learning are processes that develop over time and lead to change, so increasing the potential for improved performance, better teaching, and future learning (cf., Ambrose et al., 2010, p. 3). Music psychology research has a role to play in informing and enhancing these processes, and our authors demonstrate this in a range of musical and educational settings. Music education is also not confined to 'sound', as potentially implied by the title. Indeed, an active strand of music psychological research is to examine the varied ways in which music cognition and learning are embodied, emphasising the relevance of the body and its active interaction with the environment and others.

Context influenced teaching and research

The research reported in this book is based on studies that were conducted in England and Scotland, Spain, Portugal, and China. Naturally, the cultural contexts in these countries have influenced the research questions and findings and there might be cultural differences in attitudes to topics. For instance, in some Spanish-speaking countries it might be taboo to talk about music performance anxiety in lessons, whereas this topic is usually openly discussed in The Netherlands. In some countries it is normal educational practice to ask pupils for their opinion, whereas this might be highly unusual in other places.

Studies in this book include a range of teaching situations, from music learning in groups common in folk traditions, to instrumental lessons with children or conservatoire students, and from teaching and learning in choirs and ensembles to self-teaching of improvisation skills. Much of the focus is on the teaching of notated European classical music, but there are exceptions: Chapter 3 focuses on the aural traditions of Scottish traditional music, Chapter 6 examines the processes of learning to improvise, while Chapter 9 investigates musical signing and singing for children with hearing impairment.

For all these studies ethical approval was obtained through the standard University of Sheffield review process. Participants and their parents (in the case of children and teenagers) received information letters, had the opportunity to ask questions, and gave written or electronic informed consent. It was our intention to make research participation as inclusive as possible within the practical limitations of the projects; specifically, musicians with various abilities and levels of playing were invited to take part in these studies (see for example Chapters 3, 4, 7, 9, 10, and 11). The collection of chapters illustrates how these cultural, musical, and environmental contexts have influenced the research questions and approaches, but also invites connections across different settings, which we will return to in our closing chapter.

Research methodology

A wide variety of research methods were used by our authors, as the choice of methodology is related to the research aims and questions of each study. Several chapters report on studies that used individual or focus group interviews to learn more about participants' views on the topics under investigation (e.g., Chapters 2, 4, 7, 8). Participants ranged from young children to lifelong learners, and from new teachers to experienced music educators, who were each invited to give their perspectives in age-appropriate ways, and sometimes in native languages other than English. Thematic analysis of this qualitative data helped to illuminate the stories of lived musical experience, sometimes identifying trends in behaviours and attitudes, but more often highlighting the diversity of pupil perspectives with which any teacher, in any teaching situation, is faced. Several chapters (e.g., 2 & 8) reference Interpretative Phenomenological Analysis (IPA), which acknowledges the role of the researcher in interpreting participants' narratives, deriving themes across multiple cases, and considering the broader claims that can be made from those findings (Smith & Osborn, 2015).

Chapter 3 reports on an ethnographic case study investigating traditional music practices in Scotland while Chapter 6 describes results from Jonathan Ayerst's autoethnographic research exploring his own learning of improvisation. Ethnography is a qualitative research method based on observation and interaction with people in a real-world environment. An ethnographic approach could be viewed as research exploring unknown territory approached with open-mindedness toward events and experience, awareness of personal interaction with data, and an awareness of the researcher's own role in the musical communities they study (e.g., Ruskin & Rice, 2012). In autoethnographic studies the personal subjectivity of the researcher is central and their relationship with their own practice and situation is explored (cf., Barr, 2019). This subjective and reflective approach is extended to include perspectives from research literature on learning and development, offering a dialogue between research and practice, as well as an opportunity for scaffolded learning (Chapter 6).

The research that informed Chapters 4 and 10 employed participatory action research. In this type of research practitioners investigate an aspect of their work to understand it better or to improve it (e.g., Feldman et al., 2018). According to Cain (2012), participatory action research in education should fulfil the following conditions: it should include self-study; involve students; consider the influence of context; involve more than one action cycle; and engage with, and contribute to, the development of theory (Cain, 2012, p. 409). Mary Hawkes worked with a group of piano teachers to reflect on their own practice, implement changes, and consider the effects of these on their pupils – a cycle that, in less formal ways, offers a model for reflexive practice throughout a music educator's career. Development and process are central to action research, which differentiates it from research that aims to experimentally test the effectiveness of a certain teaching or learning approach. Experimental comparisons were done in addition to more exploratory and observational work by Henrique Meissner (Chapter 4), and Shen Li (Chapter 5). Such a mixed-methods approach is increasingly common and helps to document changes and developments over time (as in Pennill's work on socio-behavioural changes in ensembles) and participants' perspectives on these processes, as well as to verify some of their outcomes.

Overview and structure of the book

Each chapter starts with an introduction explaining the background of the study, followed by a summary of the research aims, a description of the methodology and main findings. In most chapters, the research findings are illustrated by vignettes or case studies containing practical examples or quotes. Chapters finish with a reflection on the practical implications of the research for musical development, or music learning and teaching. For ease of use, an overview of the main points is included near the end of chapters. In most chapters, 'student' is used to refer to learners at university or music college, while 'pupil' generally refers to children and amateur musicians who come to a tutor's music studio for their instrumental lessons. Whenever research participants are mentioned in chapters pseudonyms or codes are used to protect the anonymity of the people whose views are represented, except in a few cases (e.g., Chapter 9), where naming eminent professionals (with their agreement) was more respectful of their expertise.

The chapters in this book are grouped according to four themes: (1) musicians as teachers; (2) developing specialist musical skills; (3) group leadership and interaction in ensembles; and (4) strategies for enhancing musical confidence and enjoyment. The first section of the book encompasses the range of activities often included in a portfolio career. In Chapter 2 Cláudia Braz Nunes reports on a study that explored how music educators' past experiences as students influenced their current attitudes toward teaching. Findings indicate ways in which musical learning experiences impact musical lives. In various ways, music educators function as role models, shaping their students' views on music teaching as well as music performance practice. Another example of this comes in Chapter 3, where Jo Miller shares her findings from interviewing, observing, and participating with musicians in Scottish traditional music groups. Tutors in these settings are often experienced musicians who teach alongside their performing career. This chapter focuses on how tutors act as role models by constructing activities which build the skills necessary for participation in community-based traditional music sessions and informal performances.

The second section of the book addresses research related to the development of musical skills such as expression and improvisation. Expressiveness is an important aspect of music performance as it makes musical participation more enjoyable and interesting for all involved, for performers as well as listeners. Performance expression is a complex phenomenon as it is a synthesis of various elements. In an expressive performance, musicians convey an interpretation of structure, character, and associated concepts to their audience. Musical tension is also an important aspect of expressiveness; the listener should feel that the music is going somewhere (e.g., Fabian et al., 2014; Meissner, 2018). The teaching of expressive performance is explored in Chapter 4, as Henrique Meissner offers a 'toolkit' of strategies based on her research with children and teenagers. In Chapter 5 Shen Li explores the teaching of timbre, drawing on mixed-methods research which investigated interactions between body and sound for the communication of timbre in piano performances.

The last chapter in this section on specialist music skills focuses on learning improvisation skills. Although it is common for jazz musicians to improvise from the early stages of learning, there are relatively few classical musicians who learn to improvise as part of their professional education and practice. As a professional organist and pianist, Jonathan Ayerst had ample performing experience and was knowledgeable in interpreting scores. However, initially, these musicianship skills did not enable him to improvise freely on Baroque models such as Fugues and Toccatas. In Chapter 6, Ayerst describes how he learned to improvise by constructing his own exercises and by using reflective journaling to structure this developmental process.

In the third section of the book the focus is on topics related to learning in groups, group leadership, and interaction in ensembles. Playing or singing in groups is not only enjoyable, it can also be specifically formative. In Chapter 7 Nicola Pennill explores the development of communication and interaction in small ensembles across rehearsals. A longitudinal case study in a music college examined how two newly formed vocal ensembles developed toward a first performance. Pennill investigated the groups' interpersonal interactions, and their developments, highlighting the relevance of interactional behaviours at the start of a rehearsal process as well as the rapid transition and change midway through a series of rehearsals. Better understanding a group's progression toward performance can help teachers and performers to recognise and prepare for changing group dynamics over time. In Chapter 8, Michael Bonshor adds the role of the conductor to this consideration of rehearsal interactions, identifying the factors affecting confidence amongst adult amateur singers in a wide range of group singing activities, and using these research findings to extrapolate some practical recommendations for conductors working with amateur singing groups.

The final section of the book focuses on strategies for enhancing musicians' confidence and enjoyment. This section starts off with the description of an exploratory study with deaf and hearing-impaired (DHI) children who participated in singing and signing. Gail Dudson's study (Chapter 9) aimed to explore effective strategies for teaching DHI young people music skills of pitch, pulse, rhythm, and expression, and to investigate how British Sign Language can be made 'musical'. This research focused on the experience of participation, how engagement was enabled, and what activities were effective.

While many musicians have experienced music performance anxiety and there is a growing body of research investigating this phenomenon, Mary Hawkes and Elsa Perdomo-Guevara decided to focus their research on positive approaches toward performance. In Chapter 10 Hawkes considers practical applications of teaching pre-performance routines to improve pupils' performance experience. Her research shows how psychological skills training, commonplace in sport and researched in sport psychology, could also benefit musicians preparing for performance. Investigating a similar theme of enhancing performance experience, Elsa Perdomo-Guevara examined which factors may contribute to performance-related joy via a large questionnaire study with 625 professional and amateur musicians. The implications of this study for teachers are explored in Chapter 11, where Perdomo-Guevara examines teachers' roles and their acting as a first audience for their pupils, in the enhancement of students' performance experience.

We end in Chapter 12 by exploring connections between several findings and applications discussed in the book. This chapter considers implications of the reported research for lifelong music learning and future research. Readers are invited to reflect on the potential applications of these studies in the various settings of their own teaching or performing practice. We offer some strategies and suggestions for developing research skills as a music educator and reflect on the benefits of a research-informed approach for teachers and their students.

Our hope is that this book will encourage music educators, practitioners, and researchers to find the points of connection in their work, to create new opportunities to talk to one another, to engage in research, and to be inspired in their teaching and performing. It is our conviction that research is at its most powerful when embedded in and scrutinised by practice.

Notes

1 In this book 'emotion' is used in a generic sense, including affect, feeling, and mood.
2 In this book instrumental music teachers refers to voice teachers as well as instrumental teachers.

References

Ambrose, S. A., Bridges, M. W., DiPietro, M., Norman, M. K., & Lovett, M. (2010). *How learning works: Seven research-based principles for smart teaching*. Jossey-Bass.

Ashley, R., & Timmers, R. (Eds.) (2017). *The Routledge companion to music cognition*. Routledge, Taylor & Francis Group.

Barr, M. (2019). Autoethnography as pedagogy: Writing the "I" in IR. *Qualitative Inquiry, 25*(9–10), 1106–1114. https://doi.org/10.1177/1077800418792940

Cain, T. (2012). Too hard, too soft or just about right: Paradigms in music teachers' action research. *British Journal of Music Education, 29*(3), 409–425. https://doi.org/10.1017/S0265051712000290

Fabian, D., Timmers, R., & Schubert, E. (2014). *Expressiveness in music performance: Empirical approaches across styles and cultures*. Oxford University Press.

Feldman, A., Altrichter, H., Posch, P., & Somekh, B. (2018). *Teachers investigate their work: An introduction to action research across the professions* (3rd ed.). Routledge, Taylor & Francis Group.

Meissner, H. (2018). Teaching young musicians expressive performance: A mixed methods study [Doctoral dissertation, University of Sheffield]. https://etheses.whiterose.ac.uk/22929/1/THESIS_HenriqueMeissner.2018.pdf

Mills, J., & Smith, J. (2003). Teachers' beliefs about effective instrumental teaching in schools and higher education. *British Journal of Music Education, 20*(1), 5–27. https://doi.org/10.1017/S0265051702005260

Pitts, S. E. (2017). What is music education for? Understanding and fostering routes into lifelong musical engagement. *Music Education Research, 19*(2), 160–168. https://doi.org/10.1080/14613808.2016.1166196

Ruskin, J. D., & Rice, T. (2012). The individual in musical ethnography. *Ethnomusicology, 56*(F2), 299–327. https://doi.org/10.5406/ethnomusicology.56.2.0299

Smith, J. A., & Osborn, M. (2015) Interpretative phenomenological analysis. In: J. A. Smith (Ed.), *Qualitative psychology: A practical guide to research methods* (pp. 53–80). SAGE.

Sound teaching. (2018, 2019). *Sound Teaching Workshops on Expression, communication and creativity in music performance* https://www.sheffield.ac.uk/music/research/research-conferences/sound-teaching-workshops-expression-communication-and-creativity-music-performance

Part I
Musicians as teachers

2 How musical learning experiences have an impact on music educators' attitudes and practices

Cláudia Braz Nunes

Introduction

We all bring a personal history of child- and adulthood experiences that may influence how we approach situations later in life. My interest in music educators' attitudes toward teaching and how they relate to a personal or shared background arose from my experience as Portuguese music educator and music student as well as from the interviews that I conducted with conservatoire students for a Master's dissertation (Braz Nunes, 2016). These interviews showed that although each of them had different experiences in their music course, there was a common theme in their musical learning experiences. Their entire music course, like my own, was focused on becoming the best at playing an instrument and every effort was toward that goal. Later, as a music teacher, I found that this tradition of focusing on high level performance was still embedded in many Portuguese music education institutions.

Access to music education in Portugal has always been limited to specialised music institutions such as conservatoires and music academies. These specialised music institutions have a reputation for being centres of excellence with the main focus of training professional musicians (Vasconcelos, 2002). Some of my students did not respond well to the expectations of these institutions. In the first years of my career, I felt that I did not know myself as a music educator and was confused about what my role should be. Through conversations with colleagues, I realised that I was not the only one: confusion about our purpose as music educators was a common feeling.

Existing research in Portuguese music education recognises the role of the Portuguese philharmonic bands *(bandas filarmónicas)*. Philharmonic Bands are groups of amateur musicians who play in

DOI: 10.4324/9781003108382-3

ceremonies within the community. These *bandas* provide opportunities for music making that the school system does not offer. Philharmonic participants often attain high standards of musicianship which in many cases lead to a career in music (Mota, 2009).

With the aim of exploring these different routes into music education, I carried out research which focused on the importance of Portuguese music educators' narratives in understanding experiences of music education and its lifelong impact. This chapter will present one of the main themes that emerged: how music educators' learning experiences have a lasting impact on their current attitudes toward teaching.

Previous research on music teaching as a career has focused on various themes, such as reasons for choosing music education, early career challenges, music teachers' professional identities, professional development, and career aspirations (Eros, 2013; Regelski, 2007; Scheib, 2003; Welch et al., 2011). However, fewer studies explore qualitative aspects of the connections between these topics by analysing music educators' life stories and narratives (Baker, 2006; Georgii-Hemming, 2006).

Music educators' attitudes toward music education have been shown to be shaped by their experiences as students (Bouij, 1998; Dolloff, 1999; Isbell, 2008; Thompson, 2007). Thompson (2007), for example, emphasised that music educators reject aspects of the curriculum that are in conflict with their beliefs and dismiss pedagogical approaches that are different from what they have previously experienced as students.

Bouij's (1998) study was particularly relevant for the analysis of my participants' narratives. Bouij examined 169 Swedish music educators in training as they progressed through a four-year music-teaching course and into professional life. Bouij analysed the participants' transition from student and their relationship with music, to teacher and what they strived for in their teaching. Bouij's findings suggested that participants as students were characterised as either 'all-round musicians' or 'performers' and then as teachers, they became either 'pupil-centred' or 'content-centred' in their approaches to teaching. The 'pupil-centred' teacher wanted to teach music as a foundation for life and the 'content-centred' teacher aimed to teach at higher levels of performance and had little interest in developing their pupils outside the musical area (Bouij, 1998). Bouij observed that an 'all-round musician' student was more likely to become a 'pupil-centred' teacher and that a dramatic shift between a pure 'performer' to 'pupil-centred' teacher was unusual. Participants' attitudes toward music education were therefore shown to be a product of their beliefs as students.

Summary of the research

This research project was based on a life history approach which enabled the exploration of participants' early experiences, significant life transitions, external and internal influences, both professional and personal experiences as well as perceptions of those experiences (Atkinson, 1998; Goodson & Sikes, 2001). The interviews were conducted with 14 male and 12 female participants and focused on early/mid-career teachers. Early/mid-career educators were the chosen group to ensure the findings were based on the current educational system. This decision was based on the initial questionnaire responses, which showed that educators within ten years of retirement (and already retired) had views based on the old Portuguese educational system that does not exist anymore.

Since music education in Portugal has always been limited to specialised music institutions, all participants in this study had been through the specialist music course as students at some point in their lives. The prevalence of Portuguese Philharmonic Bands across the country also made these an important part of many participants' background in this study. Participants taught in various types of settings: specialised music institutions, general state schools, universities, and philharmonic associations. Participants tended to teach in more than one institution to get enough hours on their timetable. The most prevalent areas of specialism were instrumental teaching and musicianship.

The interviews were planned in a way that would cover participants' early engagement with music, their musical learning journey, their teaching journey, their views on their present career, and their future aspirations. However, many times participants would jump in time by connecting different stages of their lives throughout the interview, and their storytelling was not necessarily chronological. I did not discourage this practice, as it was important for them to make sense of their own experiences by connecting the past with the present in their narratives. The interviews were conducted in Portuguese and the interactions were casual and relaxed. Interviews took a minimum of one hour and maximum of four hours and took place in a variety of locations such as participants' homes, work, or rehearsal space. Interviews were labelled anonymously according to the participant number (1 to 26), context (F – Filarmonica/Philharmonic and/or E – Especializado/Specialised institution) and age group.

My study confirmed previous research showing that participants' attitudes toward music teaching and current teaching practices are

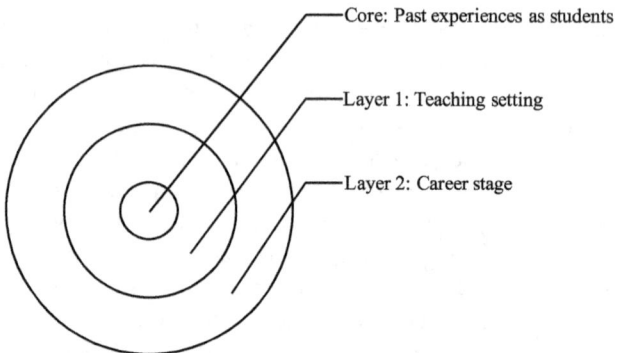

Figure 2.1 Layers of interaction affecting educators' attitudes toward music education

Source: Adapted from Braz Nunes, 2018

shaped and influenced by their previous experiences as students. However, my participants' attitudes toward music education were affected by two additional factors: their different teaching settings and their career stage (Figure 2.1).

This suggests that attitudes toward music education are constantly evolving rather than bound to previous attitudes and experiences. In the next section, these layers of interaction will be explained in more detail and illustrated with quotes from participants.

Layers of interaction affecting educators' attitudes toward music education

Past experiences as students

Similar to Bouij's study, these participants' music education experiences also resulted in two different student profiles. The first profile (16 interviewees) described memories in music education with great enthusiasm; however, they had negative and traumatic memories associated with instrumental lessons, examinations, and instrumental teachers. The comment below illustrates this profile:

> I loved everything, I especially liked my ensemble lessons and the concerts, the atmosphere [. . .] I was always afraid of Wednesdays because I had piano lessons on Wednesdays. I dreaded

Wednesdays because I knew that I was going to have to listen to my piano teacher. Because I didn't practice enough, or the practice was wrong.

(4E 18–24)

It is striking that, years later, this participant still remembered that her piano lessons were on Wednesdays and still had negative feelings associated with those lessons. Participants matching this profile decided from an early stage that they did not want to be professional performers. As a result, participants started to focus their attention and efforts on other aspects of their music course (e.g., musical analysis) and considered other career paths in music from an earlier stage in their education.

The second profile (11 interviewees) reported positive memories in their instrumental lessons, examinations, recitals, and relationship with their instrumental teacher:

On my second stage of the music course, I had 20/20 on my guitar exam, and I even celebrated [. . .] I even had fun in my guitar exams.

(24E 25–34)

These student profiles show parallels with Bouij's categorisation of All-round musician vs Performer. Furthermore, I also found correlations between student profiles and current attitudes toward music teaching (Content-centred and Pupil-centred). Participants who were confident performers as students claimed that their goal now, as music educators, was to train professional performers. As one participant said:

I think that as a teacher, what suits me is working with students who really want to learn. I like to teach students who want to become professional percussionists and that's it.

(18EF 35–44)

These participants described their teaching experiences as focusing on lesson goals, results, and exams. Furthermore, they were confident that their experiences were enough for them to be successful teachers thus not needing further pedagogical training. As one participant mentioned:

On a pedagogical level, I learnt with myself, with my experience and luckily it works.

(18EF 35–44)

On the other hand, participants who were not confident performers as students indicated that their main goal now, as educators, was to support their students in their musical learning:

> It is just understanding what is the level and the abilities of the student and where can he feel motivated. That is the challenge [. . .] Then if you are educating musicians or listeners or if you are there for personal reasons ((pause)) that is just detail. I think there is no other way of teaching other than adapting to the student.
>
> (21E 35–44)

The comment above illustrates how these teachers saw the student as the centre of their teaching. Making students feel motivated and comfortable in their learning was their priority.

Changes in attitudes influenced by participants' teaching context

Participants in this study taught in three main contexts: specialised music institutions (academies and conservatoires), philharmonic associations, and school-music. Participants teaching in specialised institutions had conflicting views on what was expected of them as music educators. Some argued that the specialised course was created to train professional musicians and that the students have to work hard to meet the expectations of the institution. Others thought that the majority of their students were not going to become professional musicians and thus they considered it more important that their students continued engaging with music making. Their views were found to be different based on their past experiences as students as analysed in the previous section. In contrast, all school educators (irrespective of student profile) agreed that their role was to promote engagement with music rather than educating high-level performers. One possible explanation for this might be the fact that music education has a precarious place in the Portuguese school curriculum; therefore, school-music teachers have to promote music learning with fewer resources. Nevertheless, school-music teachers indicated that a good teacher should be flexible and adapt their teaching:

> My greatest challenge as a music educator is being able to explain things in a way that they understand and above all in an enjoyable way. I do not want to be presumptuous, but I don't need half of

my musical knowledge to be able to teach what I teach. But on the other hand, I end up needing all of my knowledge in order to be able to meet the students' needs.

(7EF 35–44)

Curiously, all teachers from specialised institutions shared the opinion that they did not have the right profile to adjust in the way reported by school-music teachers:

> I am going to be honest with you, I love children but that type of work [. . .] it is not a job that I like to do [. . .] it is a job that personally is not my area of expertise, I'm not skilled to do it and that's it.
>
> (17E 35–44)

Specialised music teachers were trained to become professional performers and their formal training had great emphasis on virtuosity. For them, teaching outside the conservatoire system is not part of the job. It can thus be suggested that whilst specialised music teachers see their teaching practices as fixed, school-music teachers are prepared to adapt.

Philharmonic educators saw their teaching practices as a combination of their positive experiences in both specialised institutions and community philharmonic settings. Even though these settings emphasised different teaching approaches (group music-making vs one-to-one tuition). Nevertheless, their main goal was to train their students to be able to play in the band and have fun:

> First, I try so that my students see music like I used to in the band. It was not like in the conservatoire [. . .] I think that the band for me was that. It was to understand that music is not to be practised for hours until it's perfect. Music can be simply 'oops that's the wrong note but never mind'.
>
> (1EF 25–34)

Seeing enjoyment as part of the learning process was a view only mentioned by school music and Philharmonic Band teachers.

Changes in attitudes according to career stage

The majority of teachers in this study had started teaching arbitrarily. Some of them were invited to teach and others had a one-time experience and enjoyed it. In both cases, participants did not have any pedagogical training. In general, participants felt that their teaching was developed based on their teachers' influences, together with their own trial-and-error experiences. These trial-and-error experiences were challenging for some participants, leading them to almost quit this career path. Some participants referred to these first experiences as traumatic:

> That year was a death sentence, I had 350 students and I didn't even know their names. It was awful. I only knew the names of the ones who constantly misbehaved. Your expectations collide with the students' expectations. I used to arrive home crying and saying to my mum, 'I don't care! I want to work in a supermarket!'
>
> (13EF 35–44)

Participants' statements show that in those first years of their teaching careers, their main goal was to discover themselves as music teachers and to define their teaching philosophy. That goal, however, collided with what the students expected of them. This proved to be a challenging process since participants had not had the chance to teach before and everything was new for them.

The interview analysis revealed that once participants started to get more confident in their profession, they started wanting to become a role model for their students, shifting the focus of their worries from their career to their students' needs. A study with more late-career teachers might reveal more of this shift in priorities, but the four interviewees within ten years of retirement consistently saw their teaching as adaptable to the expectations of the student and the institution:

> We evaluate their expectations but not forgetting that we are the ones still in charge. And then it is funny that expectations change according to the school and that influences students' attitudes toward music learning.
>
> (25E 45–54)

These teachers have experienced many different teaching settings and developed methods to cope and adapt to different expectations. As such, their years of teaching perspectives and experiences override their perceptions as past music students.

Whilst early and mid-career teachers were focusing on developing their teaching philosophy still influenced by their past experiences as students, late-career teachers demonstrated a more critical view of their work environment. They evaluated their role within the broader context of the teaching settings that they were part of and within the opportunities provided by the educational system that they worked in.

Conclusion and implications for practice

This study indicates that music educators' attitudes have a very significant impact on their students' future engagement with music learning. Furthermore, music educators in this study reported not having pedagogical training and feeling lost in the beginning of their careers. This factor could not only put their career at risk but also affect their teaching practices. It is not surprising that previous researchers named early career years as the 'survival years' (Eros, 2013) when coping mechanisms are developed (or not) as educators gain more experience.

These findings are consistent with previous research, which suggests that music teachers look back on their education as inadequate to their current realities (Welch et al., 2011). For music education this is particularly problematic since it is widely known that being a musician does not necessarily mean being a good music teacher. This study demonstrates that participants' attitudes toward music teaching were only being developed/negotiated once they started being paid as professional music teachers. As previously mentioned by Maris (1991): 'We do not encourage children to learn to play an instrument only by trial and error, so why should we allow teachers to learn their trade that way' (p. 55).

The music educators in this study showed very different attitudes toward music education depending on their experiences and contexts. The Portuguese case offered the possibility of exploring experiences in three distinctive settings: community music, specialised music education, and school music. The analysis of participants' experiences in these settings and how those affect their current attitudes toward music provide insights for music teacher training and raise relevant questions for music educators in other countries. Should music educators support traditional music teaching practices based on the development of virtuosity? Or should educators promote opportunities for music making and facilitate access to musical engagement? How different should the music teacher be from the community music facilitator?

The analysis of music educators' experiences in community settings such as the Portuguese Philharmonic Bands could contribute in several ways to our understanding of music educators' attitudes in other countries with equivalent systems and offer new insights for those where community music is not as predominant. There is abundant room for further progress in determining how music educators' attitudes are constructed and in investigating ways to support and prepare them during this process. A reasonable approach to tackle this issue could be to encourage teachers in training to reflect not only on their current teaching but also on their past experiences as students. This type of reflection could perhaps be an effective way of gaining new insights, making links from past experiences to current practice and informing teacher training. Teacher training could also encourage awareness of teachers' attitudes toward music teaching by challenging assumptions originated in their past experiences. A starting point could be to create spaces for teachers in training to focus on themselves, share their past experiences, and solve problems together.

Main points

- Three factors were found to affect attitudes toward music education: experiences as students, teaching context, and career stage.
- Participants who were accomplished performers as students now as teachers had the main goal of training performers. Others focused on promoting musical engagement and adapting their teaching methods to their students' needs.
- Participants teaching in specialised music institutions had conflicting views on what was expected of them ranging from respecting traditional music teaching practices to a more flexible approach. For school music and Philharmonic Band educators, enjoyment was seen as essential in music learning.
- Early career teachers tended to teach in the way that they were taught and took a trial-and-error approach. Mid-career teachers shifted in focus from their needs as teachers to the needs of the students.

References

Atkinson, R. (1998). *The life story interview*. SAGE.
Baker, D. (2006). Life histories of music service teachers: The past in inductees' present. *British Journal of Music Education, 23*(1), 39–50. https://doi.org/10.1017/S026505170500673X
Bouij, C. (1998). Swedish music teachers in training and professional life. *International Journal of Music Education, 32*, 24–32. https://doi.org/10.1177/025576149803200103

Braz Nunes, C. (2016). Jovens instrumentistas e os seus hábitos de audição musical erudita. Um estudo de caso de um grupo de jovens estudantes de música, em Portugal. *Revista Portuguesa de Educação Musical, 142–143*, 27–36.

Braz Nunes, C. (2018). *Lifelong engagement with music: Learning through the lives of Portuguese music educators* [Doctoral thesis, The University of Sheffield]. http://etheses.whiterose.ac.uk/22676/1/Thesis%20Braz%20Nunes.pdf

Dolloff, L. A. (1999). Imagining ourselves as teachers: The development of teacher identity in music teacher education. *Music Education Research, 1*(2), 191–208. https://doi.org/10.1080/1461380990010206

Eros, J. (2013). Second-stage music teachers' perceptions of career development and trajectory. *Bulletin of the Council for Research in Music Education, 195*, 59–75. https://doi.org/10.5406/bulcouresmusedu.195.0059

Georgii-Hemming, E. (2006). Personal experiences and professional strategies. *Music Education Research, 8*(2), 217–236. https://doi.org/10.1080/14613800600779618

Goodson, I. F., & Sikes, P. (2001). *Life history research in educational settings: Learning from lives* (1st ed.). Open University Press.

Isbell, D. S. (2008). Musicians and teachers: The socialization and occupational identity of preservice music teachers. *Journal of Research in Music Education, 56*(2), 162–178. https://doi.org/10.1177/0022429408322853

Maris, B. E. (1991). Training musicians to teach. *American Music Teachers, 41*(2), 30–55.

Mota, G. (2009). *Crescer nas bandas filarmónicas: Um estudo sobre a construção da identidade musical de jovens portugueses*. Edições Afrontamento.

Regelski, T. A. (2007). "Music Teacher" – Meaning and practice, identity and position. *Action, Criticism, and Theory for Music Education, 6*(2), 1–35.

Scheib, J. W. (2003). Role stress in the professional life of the school music teacher: A collective case study. *Journal of Research in Music Education, 51*(2), 124–136. https://doi.org/10.2307/3345846

Thompson, L. K. (2007). Considering beliefs in learning to teach music. *Music Educators Journal, 93*(3), 30–35. https://doi.org/10.1177/002743210709300317

Vasconcelos, A. (2002). *O conservatório de música: Professores, organização e políticas*. Instituto de inovação educacional.

Welch, G. F., Purves, R., Hargreaves, D., & Marshall, N. (2011). Early career challenges in secondary school music teaching. *British Educational Research Journal, 37*(2), 285–315. https://doi.org/10.1080/01411921003596903

3   Traditional musicians as teachers

Sharing skills for participation

Josephine L. Miller

Introduction

As a young musician in the 1980s I studied in conservatoire and university settings. Most of my career, however, has been as an educator in the field of traditional music,[1] in both formal and community contexts. Playing and singing traditional music is a popular pursuit in Scotland, and substantial numbers of people learn and perform in group environments. Teachers (known as tutors) are experienced musicians, for whom this work has become a significant source of employment, often alongside a performing career. Some, like myself, have formal training, but many acquire their teaching skills through experience in community-based settings, working with learners of all ages.[2] This means of learning is popular partly because it is more financially viable than individual lessons, but equally because social experience is seen as intrinsic to the ideals of the music, and group music making provides a strong incentive for learners to progress.

The transmission of traditional music is usually defined as having two main elements: the central role played by orality and the relationship of the individual to a 'tradition', understood as a shared culture of practice.[3] These classic elements have been adapted for new environments. One such context is that of community-based organisations which operate out with formal institutions, often at a local level, are run by members pursuing similar ends, and promote participation in decision making (Miller, 2018).[4] In these respects such organisations are aligned with the democratic ideology of community music and share its participatory aims (Higgins, 2012). But groups teaching traditional music have the specific *musical* goal of learning to play an instrument (or sing or dance) via a particular repertoire and set of practices.[5] My research investigated how tutors of traditional music construct an environment in which participants acquire the skills and competencies

DOI: 10.4324/9781003108382-4

necessary to participate in social music making. I was interested in how such organisations functioned, the pedagogical strategies used by tutors, and the learning strategies used by participants, where participatory performance happened and what it sounded like, and how individuals used their agency – their ability to make choices and actions in relation to music – to continue with music making in their lives.

Summary of the research

To explore these questions, I undertook a large ethnographic case study (Miller, 2016) of a community-based organisation called Glasgow Fiddle Workshop (GFW).[6] Begun in the 1990s, and situated in Scotland's largest city, GFW has around 400 adult and junior members who attend weekly classes and activities.[7] They range from children aged eight to older people, and from complete beginners to some with established careers as professional performers and teachers. The case study approach accommodates a mix of research methods. Central to this for my purposes was the use of ethnography, a qualitative research method based on observation and interaction with people in a real-world environment. During extensive fieldwork with GFW between 2012 and 2014 (and on occasional visits since), I observed and recorded activities and conducted interviews with groups and individuals whose comments are quoted here. This chapter focuses on my analysis of GFW as a local community of practice in which tutors are 'masters', or expert members of that community (Wenger, 1998; Kenny, 2017). As learners grow in competence, they play a fuller part in the community's activities – in this case, playing traditional music. This large organisation provided the opportunity to study a diversity of activity and approaches around the teaching and learning of traditional music, and also allowed me to home in on smaller subjects such as individual biographies, a particular class, or a performance event. I want to focus here on two contexts which illustrate how GFW tutors scaffolded activities to facilitate participation: teaching skills and repertoire by ear in classes, and leading slow sessions to encourage instrumentalists to participate in performance.

Scaffolded activities to support learning and participation

The class: oral-aural learning

On the GFW website, learning 'by ear' is described as 'a method of learning often used in traditional music'. This continues: 'Scottish traditional music is part of an oral tradition which has been passed down over hundreds of years. Many of the tutors learned to play this way and find this method works really well when teaching groups of people'. There is reference here to orality as a fundamental characteristic of traditional music, but also to the pedagogical issue of how to facilitate group teaching effectively. Lastly, playing by ear offers the potential to learn more productively and be unencumbered in performance: 'As you progress with your instrument, you will be able to join in with music sessions without having to pull out lots of sheets of paper. Learning without music lets you concentrate on techniques and on the tutor more easily'.[8] 'Handy hints' give clear directions on how to get the most from classes: 'listen with your eyes and your ears. Watching the tutors is not cheating! By following their fingers, you will have a better idea of the patterns' and 'listening is almost as important as playing'.

GFW classes generally focused on one instrument, apart from 'mixed instruments' and 'ceilidh band', and class members numbered anything from a handful to over 20 musicians. The typical adult class was two hours long, including a tea break where everyone came together for announcements and socialising. In order of general popularity, there were classes for fiddle, ukulele, guitar, mandolin, accordion, whistle, mixed instrument, bodhran, banjo, cello, and ceilidh band. Junior classes in fiddle, guitar, and whistle lasted an hour, with a parents' class running alongside. Most classes were grouped according to ability – beginner, intermediate, or advanced – with tutors and participants negotiating the best 'fit'. Tutors managed a range of abilities within classes using strategies such as varying the pace of learning or offering more able players additional challenges. To some extent, members themselves regulated their own level of participation by choosing to listen or 'sit out' more difficult tunes. There was a great deal of verbal encouragement from tutors which affirmed the achievements and potential of all.

The main ingredients of classes included revising previous repertoire, learning new items, dealing with individual queries, and preparing for forthcoming events such as end-of-term gatherings. A central activity was learning new repertoire, mainly consisting of dance tunes (reels, jigs, marches, and so on, usually binary in form – AABB) for melody instruments, or songs for guitarists and ukulele players, for example. Generally, a new tune would be introduced by the tutor playing the whole piece once or twice. Presenting the piece in this way not only demonstrated the musical content but also modelled its performance by an experienced musician: 'you might play through the tune, but it's also this idea that you're putting across something about what it *is* to be playing this' (fiddle tutor). Tutors then broke the tune into phrases for the class to learn, using the terms 'echoing' and 'question and answer', and guiding them by calling out 'big jump', 'run up', or 'wee scale'. Imitation was an essential feature of teaching and learning, including the strategy of singing back phrases: 'I'll just play the first half a couple of times, then we'll just sing along to get the tune in your head first of all'; 'if you can sing a tune you can play it' (fiddle tutor). The architecture of tunes and the importance of listening and repetition was explained: 'I keep going on about the structure – how phrases keep repeating and so on. . . . it can greatly help the learning of tunes' (mandolin tutor). Although the emphasis was on learning by ear, in practice, music notation was sometimes used by both members and tutors, reflecting the norm for many traditional musicians of a mixed methods approach to learning.

GFW classes included common repertoire – well-known Scottish tunes such as 'Teribus', 'Harvest Home', and 'Atholl Highlanders' – which allowed members to play together in sessions or informal concerts. In earlier years repertoire was disseminated via recordings on cassette tapes and CDs, but since the mid-2000s, notation and audio files have been provided via the GFW website 'sessions' page.[9]

The slow session: participatory performance

The second way in which learning was scaffolded at GFW was through structured opportunities to join in participatory performances such as sessions and informal concerts, featuring a mix of instruments, melody and accompaniment, and a range of abilities. The instrumental 'session' expresses something of the ideology of traditional music as a shared and inclusive musical genre. It also represents a participatory performance where the music is (largely) 'not for listening apart from doing' (Turino, 2008, p. 52), encouraging musicians of varying ability to join in. It is important to distinguish traditional music sessions from ensembles directed by a conductor, with parts arranged and notated. While musical leadership is certainly present at sessions, the music consists of the parallel playing by ear of short tunes combined into 'sets' of several items whose sequence may not be known in advance to the performers. Slow sessions and 'teaching' sessions have become a widespread and popular feature of organised contexts for learning traditional music, and tutors often provide guidance and resources for those unfamiliar with the format.[10] During my fieldwork GFW ran a programme of graded sessions, from 'warm-ups' before class to slow sessions and a faster 'proper' session in an actual pub. The social engagement of pub sessions provided a strong motivation for many participants: 'the point here is *why* we're learning the instruments. . . . [The pub] is where you want to be, really, rather than sitting in a classroom' (mandolin player). One ukulele player explained: '[In the session] ye're playin' with other instruments and you're listenin' more. I find this more difficult [than the class], but you learn a lot from it'. The connection of sessions with licensed premises means that young musicians are largely excluded, and so most of my sources on this topic were adults. However, young people also shared their enjoyment of group making music in comments such as: 'you're playing together, and you have people on either side of you to help you. Plus, it takes the pressure off you, so you don't feel you have to get it perfect. 'Cos there's everyone else as well' (junior fiddler).[11]

Building short tunes into longer sets to create a more sustained performance is an important skill for traditional musicians but a challenging one for learners. The ability to join in 'proper' sessions was therefore a measure of GFW members' development from novice to competent musician. One tutor framed the educational role of GFW as helping people 'discover' session playing: 'if they can go somewhere and join in some of these tunes without having to scramble through their music trying to find scraps of paper, then that's what people find really inspiring'. Another said: 'people come along, and they sit and they *listen*. And that's good enough. And after a while they think "well, I've learnt a couple of tunes in my class – maybe they'll play them"', explicitly connecting oral-aural skills learned in classes to the environment of the session. Notwithstanding Turino's (2008) axiom 'not for listening but for doing', the function of listening *as* participation also plays an essential role in traditional music pedagogy.

GFW slow sessions, then, functioned as supported participatory performances where tutors usually chose the repertoire and led the playing. Tutors' function as expert role models was musically evident when they performed elaborations of tunes while the majority played the 'core' version (Turino, 2008, pp. 31–32). This is well illustrated by the following example, a performance of the reel 'Spootiskerry' (a well-known tune from the Shetland Isles) at a GFW session in the Islay Inn pub in the West End of Glasgow. Most of the performers sustain the main melody, but advanced players contribute harmonies 'formulaic variation'. This is not improvisation, but a palette of musical options constrained by the conservative structure and tonality of the

Spootiskerry

Figure 3.1 Transcription of an extract from the tune 'Spootiskerry'
Source: Adapted from Miller, 2016

tune, the steady pulse, and the maintenance of a cohesive collective sound. The extract below shows the parts being played by members and tutor respectively, as the tutor elaborates the tune by providing a counter melody, mostly a third above the tune, and varies the ends of four bar phrases (Figure 3.1).

Many aspects of GFW sessions were actively managed by tutors, as seen in this quote from the website:[12]

> Each week a slow session runs from 7:00 until 7:25 just before classes start . . . open to players of all levels to *join in or just listen. We encourage advanced players to join in with early-stage players.* . . . The tutor-led session covers tunes at a slow pace several times *so people can join in.* . . . This is *not a teaching session.* . . .

The *tutor can lead, or you can suggest a tune* for everyone to play. Each week a specific tune is featured . . . to *build up a common set* during the term.

(emphases added)

This text is prescriptive in communicating how the event works, highlighting the leadership role of tutors. These are pedagogical instructions designed to serve the GFW community. Note the implicit appeal to advanced players to step forward, thereby modelling a community with a mix of expertise, and the emphasis on contribution and participation. Music notation was regularly in use at slow sessions, either on paper or on digital devices, but this was rarely commented on by tutors. On such occasions, the value of participation appeared to be more important than strictly playing by ear, insofar as notated music could function as a stepping-stone to participation in 'proper' sessions. Slow sessions brought additional dimensions of learning to GFW, but also gave individuals the tools to participate in the wider stylistic community of practice. Gaining competence meant that those with the resources to do so could pursue music learning elsewhere in Scotland and further afield, at residential courses, festivals, or summer schools. Instrument cases often sported stickers advertising these destinations. By following the musical journeys of individuals within the organisation, we can see how they seek out further opportunities. But just as valuable is the potential for members to share music with family and friends at a local level. This can have a significant impact for local venues and events, thereby contributing to the cultural vitality of the area. GFW and its satellite groups have done this through performances, workshops, and ceilidhs in central Scotland since the mid-1990s.

Conclusion and implications for practice

As my ethnographic analysis has shown, GFW promotes an ethos of participation which permeates all its activities. This is partly a result of the ideology of traditional music as a social music, but also a pragmatic response to the challenges of teaching mixed ability groups. Many professional traditional musicians have built a community of adherents who not only attend their gigs but also become their students. In community-based organisations such as Glasgow Fiddle Workshop, tutors scaffold learning to help members to become competent on their instruments, to join in activities there, and to direct their own musical development in the longer term. Oral-aural learning and teaching, for instance, not only puts the focus on the tutor's role as 'master' but encourages listening skills which equips participants to go on their own musical journeys: 'I do like learning by ear – it really helps me, because if I hear a tune off a CD, I can pick it up then' (fiddle player). This is a good illustration of 'purposive listening', where 'the learner has the conscious purpose of copying or in some other way putting to practical instrumental use, the music to which they are listening' (Smart & Green, 2017, p. 433). The oral-aural dimension (including digital spheres) features in the transmission of music in many cultures, and music educators who are interested in 'world music pedagogy' have also made 'engaged listening' fundamental to their practice (Campbell, 2016). As GFW's 'handy hints' concludes, 'Learning by ear is a skill which improves the more you do it'. Using such strategies, musicians could progress through increasingly challenging contexts, expanding the traditional concept of apprenticeship from a master/student relationship to 'one of changing participation and identity transformation in a community of practice' (Wenger, 1998, p. 11).

How do tutors learn to direct and facilitate such activity? For many (including myself), it is a matter of learning 'on the job', by trial and error and sharing experience with colleagues. Here, I have focused on oral-aural learning and teaching strategies, and the participatory performance format of slow sessions. The main role of the tutor of traditional music is to model learning, but in addition, they respect the various motivations participants bring to the group, harnessing the existing musical and leadership skills of able members to sustain the organisation. Research in the areas indicated in this chapter contributes to an understanding of what traditional musicians regard as necessary for competence in their music culture, but also offers a resource for other practitioners interested in facilitating participatory music making. Musicians of all genres may wish to reflect on the role of sociality in their own musical lives and those of their students, the extent to which this can – or should – be encouraged, and strategies for doing so.

Main points

- *Listening* plays a valuable role in music learning: using 'purposive listening', short tunes can be taught by modelling a phrase at a time which is then repeated cumulatively by students.
- Teaching *common repertoire* to several students, or groups, can facilitate social music making through opportunities to play this repertoire together outside the context of classes.

32 Josephine L. Miller

- Encouraging more skilled players to *add something to the music* appropriate to the idiom can help to build creative skills in using ornaments, harmonies, or variation.
- Teachers can help students by observing and discussing the variety of *learning strategies*: tutor as role model, recordings, notation, and assisting each other.
- Tutors in a community-based organisation have a responsibility to create a supportive environment for learning, and a role to play in facilitating connections with the wider local musical culture.

Notes

1 The term traditional (rather than folk) music is commonly used in Scotland, often shortened to 'trad'.
2 I have theorised this as a 'pedagogy of participation' in Miller (forthcoming).
3 For convenience and customary usage, 'oral' is often employed to signify both transmission and hearing, not to mention visual elements. Since this chapter discusses listening, I use the term oral-aural.
4 I have avoided the 'non-formal' designation, which seems to me unhelpful in this context because of its lack of focus on how individuals actually learn.
5 Dance and song are closely related to (and often taught alongside) instrumental music, but my focus here is on the latter.
6 It may be helpful to supply some background to the emergence of groups such as GFW. Firstly, following the folk revival of the 1950s–1960s, there is now a thriving commercial scene for traditional musicians with audiences keen not only to attend gigs but also to learn the music. This is part of a transnational community of practice connecting 'Celtic' nations like Scotland and Ireland with North America and others (Gilbert, 2018). Secondly, since the 1970s participation in the arts generally has expanded. Thirdly, in Scotland the establishment of a devolved parliament in 1997 directed new public policy and funding towards third sector organisations. Lastly, the incorporation of traditional music into formal education has led to increasing focus on pedagogies of traditional and other 'non-canonical' musics in schools, colleges, universities, and conservatoires.
7 Since 2017 the organisation has renamed itself 'Glasgow Folk-Music Workshop' to take account of the wide range of instruments now taught, but retains the acronym GFW https://gfw.scot/
8 https://gfw.scot/learning-gfw (accessed 1 July 2020).
9 https://gfw.scot/gfw-sessions The current range of GFW sessions can be seen here (accessed 29 June 2020).
10 See, for example, www.nigelgatherer.com/sess/sss.html and many international examples.
11 Traditional music activities aimed at young people do often use the session format as an educational tool. On the (gendered) association of traditional music with pubs, see O'Shea (2008), and on the pleasures of

sessions at home and other more intimate contexts for music making, see McKerrell (2016).
12 https://gfw.scot/learning-gfw (accessed 1 July 2020)

References

Campbell, P. S. (2016). World music pedagogy: Where music meets culture in classroom practice. In C. R. Abril & B. M. Gault (Eds.), *Teaching general music: Approaches, issues, and viewpoints* (pp. 90–112). Oxford University Press.

Gilbert, L. (2018). 'Not just bow and string and notes': Directors' perspectives on community building as pedagogy in Celtic traditional music education organizations. *International Journal of Music Education, 36*(4), 588–600. https://doi.org/10.1177/0255761418774938

Higgins, L. (2012). *Community music in theory and practice.* Oxford University Press.

Kenny, A. (2017). *Communities of musical practice.* Routledge.

McKerrell, S. (2016). *Focus: Scottish traditional music.* Routledge.

Miller, J. L. (2016). *An ethnographic analysis of learning, participation and agency in a Scottish traditional music organisation* [Doctoral thesis, The University of Sheffield]. http://etheses.whiterose.ac.uk/14286/

Miller, J. L. (2018). 'A sense of who we are': The cultural value of community-based traditional music in Scotland. In S. McKerrell & G. West (Eds.), *Understanding Scotland musically: folk, tradition and policy* (pp. 30–43). Routledge.

Miller, J. L. (Forthcoming). *A pedagogy of participation: Community-based traditional music in Scotland.* Routledge.

O'Shea, H. (2008). *The making of Irish traditional music.* Cork University Press.

Smart, T., & Green, L. (2017). Informal learning and musical performance. In J. Rink, H. Gaunt, & A. Williamon (Eds.) *Musicians in the making: Pathways to creative performance. Vol. 1 of Studies in musical performance as creative practice* (pp. 108–125). Oxford University Press.

Turino, T. (2008). *Music as social life: The politics of participation.* University of Chicago Press.

Wenger, E. (1998). *Communities of practice: Learning, meaning and doing.* Cambridge University Press.

Part II
Developing specialist musical skills

4 Teaching children and teenagers expressive music performance

Henrique Meissner

Introduction

My interest in teaching performance expression to young musicians stems from my experience as a recorder teacher. When I started teaching, I held the common assumption that some children are more 'musical' than others; I thought that some might have a talent for performing expressively while others might not be able to play convincingly. However, over the years I have seen many pupils improve their expressiveness; children who initially were quite 'wooden' players became engaging musicians, some even winning prizes in local music competitions or acquiring music scholarships in their teenage years. Although the rate of learning and intensity of expressiveness varied, most pupils were able to develop their performance expression. Following these experiences, I became intrigued by the process of teaching and learning expressiveness. How do children learn to perform expressively, and how can we teach expressiveness effectively? Therefore, I decided to explore how instrumental teachers can facilitate young musicians' learning of expressive performance.

In this chapter I will first give a brief summary of literature related to performance expression and teaching and learning of expressiveness. Next, I will describe the main findings of my research with 54 pupils aged 8–16 in various projects. These musicians received weekly instrumental music tuition but were not studying at a specialist music school or junior academy and had no known special educational needs. In my research I used various methodologies: participatory action research involving other teachers and their pupils; an experimental study comparing the outcome of a lesson using dialogic teaching of expressiveness with a control lesson focusing on accuracy and technique; and a qualitative study consisting of questionnaires and video-stimulated recall interviews. These mixed methods allowed me to explore in depth young musicians' experiences of learning and practising expressive performance.

Interpretation and expressive performance

Although the notation that is traditionally used for European art music contains a representation of pitch and rhythm, it cannot represent everything that is required for an expressive performance (e.g., Howat, 1995). Some musicians might intend to let a score 'speak for itself' while others will focus more on their interpretation of the structure and character of a composition. The interpretation of the musical meaning of a work tends to vary depending on the performer, listener, and situation (Silverman, 2007). Music psychology research has demonstrated that various expressive 'tools' such as articulation, dynamics, tempo, timbre, timing, and ornamentation can be used to convey the structure of a musical work (e.g., Clarke, 1988; Palmer, 1996). Furthermore, researchers have shown that expressive tools can be used to communicate character, affect, or emotion in performance (e.g., Gabrielsson, 1999; Timmers & Ashley, 2007). Other aspects are important too – for example, playing with musical tension and expressive intensity (e.g., Nusseck & Wanderley, 2009) or giving a stylish performance following appropriate stylistic conventions (Schubert & Fabian, 2014).

Teaching and learning expressive performance

Research conducted with adults or students in tertiary education has found that aural modelling, verbal teaching using metaphors, verbal teaching explaining musical properties, a focus on felt emotion, and constructive feedback can be effective methods for improving musicians' expressiveness (e.g., Woody, 2003, 2006; Van Zijl & Sloboda, 2011). Studies conducted with young musicians have found that children tend to focus on technique and reading during practice (e.g., Lisboa, 2008; Pitts et al., 2000) and that various strategies can be used to enhance children's expressiveness such as modelling, metaphors, gestures, work on phrasing, or listening back to pupils' recordings (see Brenner & Strand, 2013; McPhee, 2011). Research with teenage choristers indicated that problem-solving activities may be useful for developing expressiveness (Broomhead, 2005). Generally, these were projects with small groups of participants, leaving scope for further research.

Summary of the research: dialogic teaching and modelling at the heart of teaching and learning expressiveness

For my research projects I defined an expressive music performance as a performance in which the musician communicates their interpretation of the musical character and structure convincingly to a listener. The *musical character* relates to the atmosphere, feelings, or movement that may be represented in a musical work (see Shaffer, 1995). Conveying both the structure and the character of the music is important for creating a convincing performance.

I started my research by investigating methods for teaching expressiveness together with eight colleagues (professional musicians and teachers) and 14 pupils in an action research project (Meissner, 2017). In action research in education, teachers explore an aspect of their practice to improve it or to understand it better (e.g., Feldman et al., 2018). For ten weeks we explored methods for facilitating children's learning of expressiveness. We found that various methods can be used for working on expressiveness with children: gestures and movements or drama to explore the musical character; thinking of visual imagery to describe the music; modelling, i.e., playing for pupils or listening to recordings; listening with pupils to their own recorded performances; or asking questions about the music's character and structure and talking about this with pupils. At the end of the project the participating tutors thought that all these methods had been effective during lessons. However, analysis of performance assessment scores did not show a significant improvement of expressiveness. Notably, four out of five pupils who did improve their expressiveness were taught by tutors who had used enquiry and discussion of the musical character.

Therefore, I decided to explore the effectiveness of 'dialogic teaching' further in an experimental study with 29 participants. In dialogic teaching, tutors ask open questions rather than telling learners what to do (Alexander, 2008). In a dialogic teaching approach for working on performance expression, teachers ask learners for their views on the character and structure of the music. Usually, a conversation follows in which teachers and learners discuss their ideas. For instance, teachers may ask 'What is the character of this composition?' or 'What is the structure of this piece?'

In the experimental study participants were given two contrasting test pieces, one in a major key with a 'happy' character, and another in a minor key with a 'sad' character. Control group participants worked on accuracy and fluency in playing through scales practice, practice of difficult sections, and improvisation using rhythmic or melodic patterns from the test piece. Experimental group participants first worked on accuracy and fluency. Subsequently, I asked 'What is the character of this music?' This question led to a conversation about the musical character and how this can be conveyed in playing. The questions and conversation affected participants' playing. Adjudicators' assessment scores demonstrated that their rendition of the 'sad' piece, especially, sounded more expressive, fluent, and accurate than performances of this piece by participants in the control group (Meissner & Timmers, 2019).

Afterwards, reports from participants in the experimental group demonstrated that the questions concerning the character had helped them to think about the music. They had become aware of the musical character and how the feeling of the music can be conveyed in playing (Meissner et al., 2020). In a subsequent action research study, I investigated this further, together with four colleagues and 11 pupils. We explored the use of questions about the musical character, aural modelling (playing for pupils), and playing along with pupils. This study confirmed that asking questions about the musical character can be useful for teaching and learning of expressiveness. We found that modelling is important too, and that this can be especially effective when it is combined with questions and discussion about the music.

Several teachers in my studies noticed that children and teenagers have perceptive ideas about the music they are playing. Some teachers were really impressed by pupils' understanding. When teachers asked pupils for their view of the musical character, the children started reflecting on the feeling of the music and this immediately helped them to play more expressively. Additionally, teachers asked learners *how* they can convey the character of the music. What can the musician do with articulation, dynamics, tempo, or tone colour to convey the musical character? Participants explained how questions about the musical character had helped them to consider the meaning of a composition (Meissner et al., 2020). This had helped them to reflect on and convey the musical meaning in their playing.

In addition, pupils and teachers found modelling useful; they reported that it is helpful when a teacher plays for their pupil or when teachers and learners listen to recordings together. Teachers' demonstrations or listening to recordings can help pupils to get an 'aural picture' of what the music may sound like (e.g., Hallam, 1998). This can be helpful for children's learning of rhythm or pitch, and it can also be useful for exploring various interpretations of a composition (Meissner & Timmers, 2020). Teachers can model various interpretations of a work or teachers and learners can listen to different recordings together and discuss these: Which version do they prefer and why? What did the musician do to create this performance?

One teacher in my last action research study thought that modelling was especially important for pupils who were in the early stages of learning or had technical difficulties. His pupils, who had struggled with pitch and pulse, especially benefited from aural modelling or someone playing along with them. Contrastingly, other teachers in this project thought that dialogic teaching supported by modelling can be used even from the beginning stages of learning a piece. Additionally, they had observed that focusing on the musical character can have a positive effect on learners' accuracy and technique.

In this last action research project, we explored mainly the use of questions and dialogue combined with modelling and playing along to facilitate learners' learning of expressiveness. Although other methods, such as gestures and movements, projected performance, or listening to their own recordings had not been investigated systematically during this project, participating tutors thought that these strategies could be used within a dialogic teaching approach too. Even so, most tutors thought that dialogic teaching combined with modelling is central for teaching and learning of expressive performance, and that instruction should always be tailored to the student and the situation.

Rationale for using dialogic teaching in combination with modelling

Learning to play a musical instrument is a challenging activity. It seems likely that children tend to focus on technique and note reading in their practice (e.g., Lisboa, 2008; Pitts et al., 2000) because of the difficulties of instrumental music learning (Meissner, 2018). Additionally, some research suggests that tutors may focus predominantly on note reading and technical issues in music lessons (Karlsson & Juslin, 2008; McPherson et al., 2012; West & Rostvall, 2003), which may well hinder children's expressiveness. When teachers start asking questions about the character of the music, these questions shift the child's focus from note reading or technical issues to the interpretation of a work. Reflection on the interpretation and awareness of the musical character are fundamental for the development of children's expressiveness in performance.

Vignettes illustrating a dialogic teaching approach for enhancing expressiveness

Eloise, a nine-year-old violinist, was keen to participate in the research project and had practised her test pieces carefully. At the start of her experimental session, she played her pieces quickly and confidently, using the same tempo and articulation for the 'sad' piece, Rain, as for the 'happy' piece, Branle. After work on tuning and accuracy by practising scales and some passages that seemed difficult for her, I asked Eloise: 'What is the feeling of this piece?' Her facial expression changed immediately, and in a soft voice she replied 'sad'. I asked her whether she could convey this in her playing. She nodded and immediately started playing softer, slower, and more legato, which resulted in an expressive performance that was moving and much more convincing than her playing at the start of the session.

Brass teacher Tim modelled a deadpan version of a piece for 14-year-old Lucy (French horn) and said:

Tim: It is all very nice, and all the right notes and rhythms wasn't it?
Lucy: Yah ((nodding))
Tim: There's nothing wrong with it you might say.
Lucy: It needs a bit more *character* ((gestures))
Tim: *Absolutely*. What kind of character would you say this piece is?
Lucy: Ehm . . . it's more like *standing out*, it's more ((hesitant, gestures))
Tim: Standing out? Interesting that, good.
Lucy: I don't know.
Tim: Anything else to describe the character?
Lucy: Ehm, more fierce . . . and to make it like . . .
Tim: *Fierce?*
Lucy: No . . . ((gesturing))
Tim: There is no right or wrong answer, that's the thing; it's kind of the character you want to make it.

Afterwards, I asked Lucy in a video-stimulated recall interview what had been special for her music learning during the research project. She replied:

> I think . . . I think . . . it's just like . . . we said more about character, more about like the moment ((hesitantly)) and the, ehm ((humming)) I don't know how to explain it, the atmosphere and how it should be played, and not how I played it. . . .

Lucy was looking for the right words to describe how the teaching and reflecting made a difference to her playing. Lucy makes a distinction between 'how I played it' and 'how it should be played'. Tim's comment to Lucy– 'there is no right or wrong answer' – was important for her too, as she needed encouragement that her views were relevant. Afterwards, several tutors mentioned that it is important to emphasise that there is no wrong answer to questions about the interpretation of musical character but rather that learners need to reflect on the meaning of their music for them personally.

Conclusion and implications for teaching practice

The research findings reported above demonstrate that it is possible to teach children performance expression. Playing convincingly is not an innate ability but a skill that can be learned. Compositions can have various interpretations and even young children might have their own ideas about a musical work, which may be different from their teachers'. As interpretations can vary, it is important to ask open questions about the musical character. When teachers ask genuine questions and are open to pupils' ideas, they stimulate their pupils' thinking about the music, which will help to develop their musical understanding. It may be difficult to accept some of the more unusual interpretations that a child might offer but being open to doing so can make teaching more interesting and rewarding.

Teaching expressiveness is possible from the early stages of learning. Young children can already think about the feeling they would like to convey in their playing. They can consider the musical character of pieces they play from notation or of pieces they improvise. For instance, they can be asked to improvise a happy, dance-like piece or a piece conveying sadness or anger.

If children are encouraged to think about the musical meaning of their pieces from the beginning, this will probably make their music learning more interesting and 'relatable'. They can make the piece they are learning 'their own' and this is likely to enhance their motivation and enjoyment. My research has shown that it is unnecessary to wait until a child can play a piece accurately before working on expressiveness. It is possible to ask questions about the feeling of a piece from the beginning stages of learning it. Thinking about the musical character and aiming to convey this in performance can even help to play more accurately and fluently (Meissner & Timmers, 2019, 2020).

44 Henrique Meissner

Furthermore, modelling is important for young musicians' learning. Hearing a piece helps with knowing what to aim for during practice. Several colleagues mentioned that they had avoided modelling in the past as they thought that this might hinder the development of pupils' sight-reading skills. However, sight-reading can be practised separately using exercises that are easier than learners' current level of playing. Other colleagues were concerned that modelling might inhibit pupils' thinking about their own interpretation. However, this does not need to be the case when teachers combine modelling with questions and discussion about the interpretation. Additionally, teachers and pupils could explore various interpretations by listening to recordings and discussing different renditions of a work.

Teachers can use various methods complementing the teacher-pupil dialogue about character and structure, such as movements and gestures, visual imagery, focusing on a 'projected performance' or imagined emotion. All these methods can be used to explore the musical character or structure further. Movements, for example, can be used to express the feeling or direction of the music, or children can be invited to project their interpretation of a work to an imaginary audience (Figure 4.1).

Although tutors observed that asking questions and modelling had been effective for improving pupils' expressiveness during lessons, teachers noticed that expressiveness had not yet improved in performances due to performance anxiety. Even though performance

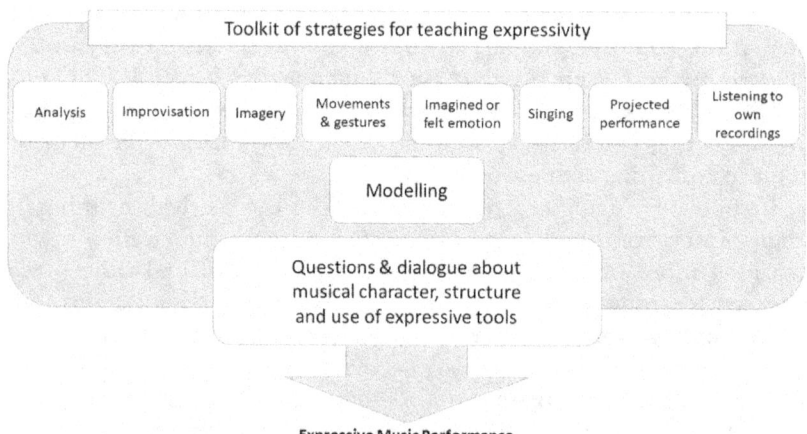

Figure 4.1 'Toolkit' of strategies for teaching expressive music performance
Source: Meissner, 2021

sessions had been informal small-scale events, performing had raised anxiety levels, especially for the teenagers in this study. For several teenagers it had been a new experience to perform for an audience. These students reported that this had made them nervous, while at the same time they had found it helpful to perform several times within a fairly short time frame. It seems therefore, that it is important to practise performing too (Meissner, 2021; see also Chapter 10).

In conclusion, open questions and dialogue about the musical character and structure are at the heart of teaching and learning expressiveness. It is important to ask genuine questions and to be open to learners' interpretation. Questions about the musical character can stimulate learners' thinking, thus enhancing their expressiveness. Modelling is also essential for children's development of expressiveness, as this helps to build up an aural picture of the music. Teachers can work with young musicians on performance expression from the early stages of learning. Developing a personal interpretation and conveying this in performance is likely to enhance children's expressiveness, motivation, and enjoyment in music participation.

Main points

- Expressiveness can be developed from the early stages of learning.
- Asking open questions is at the heart of teaching expressiveness.
- Modelling is useful for improving accuracy as well as expressiveness.
- Children often have perceptive ideas about a musical work.
- It is useful to practise performing for a friendly audience.

References

Alexander, R. (2008). *Towards dialogic teaching: Rethinking classroom talk* (4th ed.). Dialogos UK Ltd.

Brenner, B., & Strand, K. (2013). A case study of teaching musical expression to young performers. *Journal of Research in Music Education, 61*(1), 80–96. https://doi.org/10.1177/0022429412474826

Broomhead, P. (2005). Shaping expressive performance: A problem-solving approach. *Music Educators Journal, 91*(5), 63. https://doi.org/10.2307/3400145

Clarke, E. F. (1988). Generative principles in music performance. In J. A. Sloboda (Ed.), *Generative processes in music: The psychology of performance, improvisation, and composition* (pp. 1–26). Clarendon Press/Oxford University.

Feldman, A., Altrichter, H., Posch, P., & Somekh, B. (2018). *Teachers investigate their work: An introduction to action research across the professions* (3rd ed.). Routledge, Taylor & Francis Group.

Gabrielsson, A. (1999). Studying emotional expression in music performance. *Bulletin of the Council for Research in Music Education, 141*, 47–53. www.jstor.org/stable/40318983

Hallam, S. (1998). *Instrumental teaching: A practical guide to better teaching and learning*. Heinemann Educational.

Howat, R. (1995). What do we perform? In J. Rink (Ed.), *The practice of performance: Studies in musical interpretation* (pp. 3–20). Cambridge University Press.

Karlsson, J., & Juslin, P. N. (2008). Musical expression: An observational study of instrumental teaching. *Psychology of Music, 36*(3), 309–334. https://doi.org/10.1177/0305735607086040

Lisboa, T. (2008). Action and thought in cello playing: An investigation of children's practice and performance. *International Journal of Music Education, 26*(3), 243–267. https://doi.org/10.1177/0255761408092526

McPhee, E. A. (2011). Finding the muse: Teaching musical expression to adolescents in the one-to-one studio environment. *International Journal of Music Education, 29*(4), 333–346. https://doi.org/10.1177/0255761411421084

McPherson, G. E., Davidson, J. W., & Faulkner, R. (2012). *Music in our lives: Rethinking musical ability, development, and identity*. Oxford University Press.

Meissner, H. (2017). Instrumental teachers' instructional strategies for facilitating children's learning of expressive music performance: An exploratory study. *International Journal of Music Education, 35*(1), 118–135. https://doi.org/10.1177/0255761416643850

Meissner, H. (2018). *Teaching young musicians expressive performance: A mixed methods study* [Doctoral thesis, The University of Sheffield]. http://etheses.whiterose.ac.uk/22929/1/THESIS_HenriqueMeissner.2018.pdf

Meissner, H. (2021). A theoretical framework for facilitating young musicians' learning of expressive performance. *Frontiers in Psychology, 11*, 584171. https://doi.org/10.3389/fpsyg.2020.584171

Meissner, H., & Timmers, R. (2019). Teaching young musicians expressive performance: An experimental study. *Music Education Research, 21*(1), 20–39. https://doi.org/10.1080/14613808.2018.1465031

Meissner, H., & Timmers, R. (2020). Young musicians' learning of expressive performance: The importance of dialogic teaching and modeling. *Frontiers in Education, 5*, 11. https://doi.org/10.3389/feduc.2020.00011

Meissner, H., Timmers, R., & Pitts, S. (2020). "Just notes": Young musicians' perspectives on learning expressive performance. *Research Studies in Music Education, 11*, 652–680. https://doi.org/10.1177/1321103X19899171

Nusseck, M., & Wanderley, M. M. (2009). Music and motion – How music-related ancillary body movements contribute to the experience of music. *Music Perception: An Interdisciplinary Journal, 26*(4), 335–353. https://doi.org/10.1525/mp.2009.26.4.335

Palmer, C. (1996). On the assignment of structure in music performance. *Music Perception: An Interdisciplinary Journal, 14*(1), 23–56. https://doi.org/10.2307/40285708

Pitts, S. E., Davidson, J. W., & McPherson, G. E. (2000). Models of success and failure in instrumental learning: Case studies of young players in the first 20 months of learning. *Bulletin of the Council for Research in Music Education*, *146*, 51–69. www.jstor.org/stable/40319033

Schubert, E., & Fabian, D. (2014). A taxonomy of listeners' judgements of expressiveness in music performance. In D. Fabian, R. Timmers, & E. Schubert (Eds.), *Expressiveness in music performance: Empirical approaches across styles and cultures* (pp. 283–303). Oxford University Press.

Shaffer, L. H. (1995). Musical performance as interpretation. *Psychology of Music*, *23*(1), 17–38. https://doi.org/10.1177/0305735695231002

Silverman, D. (2013). *Doing qualitative research* (3rd ed.). SAGE.

Silverman, M. (2007). Musical interpretation: Philosophical and practical issues. *International Journal of Music Education*, *25*(2), 101–117. https://doi.org/10.1177/0255761407079950

Timmers, R., & Ashley, R. (2007). Emotional ornamentation in performances of a Handel sonata. *Music Perception*, *25*(2), 117–134. https://doi.org/10.1525/mp.2007.25.2.117

Van Zijl, A. G. W., & Sloboda, J. (2011). Performers' experienced emotions in the construction of expressive musical performance: An exploratory investigation. *Psychology of Music*, *39*(2), 196–219. https://doi.org/10.1177/0305735610373563

West, T., & Rostvall, A.-L. (2003). A study of interaction and learning in instrumental teaching. *International Journal of Music Education*, *40*(1), 16–27. https://doi.org/10.1177/025576140304000103

Woody, R. H. (2003). Explaining expressive performance: Component cognitive skills in an aural modeling task. *Journal of Research in Music Education*, *51*(1), 51–63. https://doi.org/10.2307/3345648

Woody, R. H. (2006). The effect of various instructional conditions on expressive music performance. *Journal of Research in Music Education*, *54*(1), 21–36. https://doi.org/10.1177/002242940605400103

5 Developing timbre on the piano
Interactions between sound, body, and concepts

Shen Li

Introduction

Timbre is often seen as purely related to sound. It has been defined as 'that attribute of auditory sensation' that enables listeners to 'judge that two sounds similarly presented [with] the same loudness and pitch are dissimilar' (American National Standards Institue, 1973, p. 56). However, the idea that timbre is restricted to variations in sounds is not applicable to piano performance, as the variation of piano timbre is limited and greatly depends on the performed intensity (Ortmann, 1925; Turner, 1939). Nevertheless, pianists claim to vary timbre in their performances. It might be that the awareness of timbre in music is a matter of body and sound, and that timbre could be perceived both aurally and visually (Parncutt & Troup, 2002; Doğantan-Dack, 2011; Traube, 2004). I conducted a series of studies that explored the multidimensionality of timbre and investigated it as a concept that integrates body and mind. The research addressed questions that I had been considering from an early stage in my piano learning.

When I was learning the piano, one of the most challenging things in a lesson was to answer my tutor's questions related to timbre: 'Could you hear the differences between these two sounds?' To be honest, I lacked the aural sensitivity in sound until my teacher corrected my performance and demonstrated that my sounds were too harsh. This is because my conception of piano timbre was unidimensional and stayed at a basic level – timbre meant either louder or softer sounds, longer or shorter notes to me at that time. I found it hard to understand the timbre descriptors (e.g., bright, round, rich or deep tone) that my teacher often used in the lessons. Although later I became more accomplished in performance, a motivation to understand in greater depth what timbre means for pianists and how it can be manipulated stayed with me and became the focal point of my research.

DOI: 10.4324/9781003108382-7

Summary of the research

To investigate how pianists conceptualise the notion of piano timbre, I interviewed eight pianists from the Department of Music at the University of Sheffield about their use of timbre and asked them to illustrate their conceptualisations on the piano (this study is reported in Li & Timmers, 2020). Subsequently, I conducted a perceptual experiment in which 21 listeners (piano students) judged the timbre of 18 performances with varied timbral characteristics that were presented as sound-only, vision-only, or both. This tested whether visual aspects of performance indeed influence piano timbre perception. Finally, I observed nine piano lessons in which three pairs of teachers and students participated at Henan University (China) and coded their behaviours and the vocabularies used to communicate concepts and intentions related to piano timbre.

A holistic experience of piano timbre

During the interviews, pianists explained their understanding of piano timbre as something inseparable from the interpretation of a musical work and its compositional structures. Piano timbre was conceived in a holistic manner as the sum of performance parameters and interacting with compositional elements such as musical style and structure. For example, pianist 1 (P1) indicated her understanding of timbre as the 'acoustic journey of loudness and softness'; while pianist 5 (P5) related timbre to other musical parameters such as 'melodic contour, music fluidity, and breath in a phrase'.

The pianists referred to a multitude of modalities when explaining their intended timbre, indicating that piano timbre is a blended concept that results from a merging of performative action, metaphorical images, and the intended sound (see Vignette 1). For example, 'a violin timbre on the piano' is a blending between violin sound and performance gestures applied to the piano. Central to the blended concept of piano timbre is the embodied experience when perceiving and producing timbre. When realising a timbre, performers establish a strong association between proprioceptive[1] sensations and the subjective experience of the produced timbre, during which the bodily experiences such as weight, tension, relaxation, and movement direction are integrated with the experience of piano sounds. Mind and body work together in the production of piano timbre, and characteristics of the performing body become a basis informing perception and performance. For example, several pianists associated bodily feelings of weak and loose with 'hollow' sound, and related restrained and firm hands to a 'firm and strong' sound. These movements do not merely differentiate playing techniques but are closely coupled to the impression of timbre. As Doğantan-Dack (2011) suggested, the performer's gestures can form their subjective experience of tone production; they may experience piano timbre from the beginning of the fixating gestures before the tone starts sounding.

The above statements about piano timbre are distinct from the established definition of timbre, indicating that the concept of timbre is not merely variations in sounds, but a matter of sound *and* body. If we take a closer look at the acoustical attributes of piano sounds, the results might be disappointing for pianists. Several acousticians have systematically controlled the influence of other variables (intensity, duration, pitch) and investigated the role of touch qualities on tone production (Ortmann, 1925; Turner, 1939). They found that pianists have little control over the produced piano timbre when intensity is kept constant. The only elements that can be varied are the attack noises of finger-key strikes and key-keyframe strikes (i.e., when the key reaches key-bottom), which are subtle variations as listeners find it challenging to detect such changes (Goebl, Bresin, & Fujinaga, 2014).

In other words, there is a seeming contradiction between acoustical perspectives on piano timbre and pianists' conception of touch-tone relationships: as performers, pianists are taught and trained for many years to improve playing techniques in order to obtain timbral nuances in piano performance. Intriguingly, musicians do not seem to be bothered by acousticians' or scientists' perspectives (Parncutt & Troup, 2002). The difference may arise from their contrasting approaches. Physicists are concerned with the timbre of isolated piano tones. Instead, pianists consider the production of timbre in a polyphonic and melodic context: they seldom play music with a single tone, and they do not necessarily face the challenge of how to vary timbre while keeping the same intensity and duration. Their actual challenge is to manage the texture and interplay of various performance parameters (e.g., timing, dynamics, timbre, and articulation), and to consider timbre production in a musical context where communication and expression are at the centre of the performance. They may include other communicative components such as imagery and bodily expression that acoustic examination alone would fail to discover. Additionally, what pianists are concerned with is the impact of different interpretations, understandings, and playing techniques, as a result of which changes of concurrent intensity, as well as temporal features, all belong to the category of changing timbre.

Timbre can be perceived both aurally and visually

The perceptual experiment demonstrated that visual information indeed affects listeners' perception of piano timbre, in addition to auditory information. The figure below (Figure 5.1) shows the example of listeners' timbre perception in three audio-visual conditions (seeing-only, both seeing and hearing, and hearing-only). The results indicate that when visual information is included, listeners can better differentiate contrasting intentions as the distance between the mean ratings is larger when visual information is included.

Movement is not only responsible for producing sounds; it also has a communicative function between performers and their audience. Performers' gestures not only refine and modify sound-production, but also convey intentions. As pianist Charles Rosen (2002, p.30) indicated,

> I do not wish to defend the more extravagant gestures, but I have found that even the most emphatic final cadence will sometimes not convince an audience that the music is finished; without some

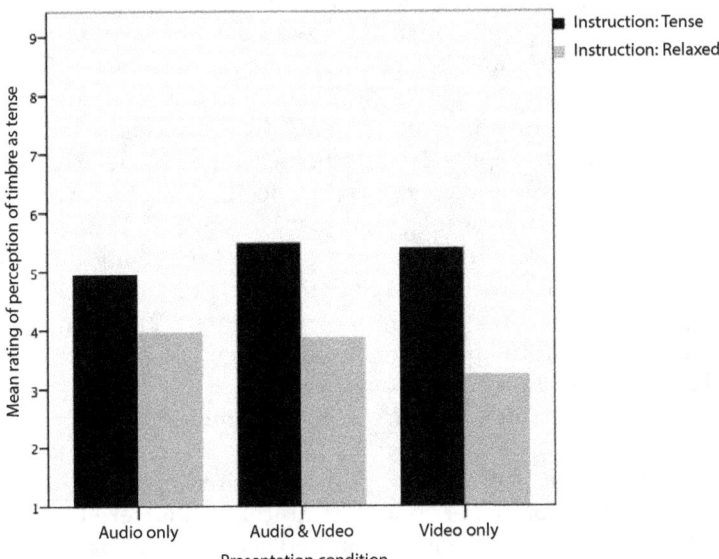

Figure 5.1 The perception of piano timbre to be tense for performances performed under the instruction of 'tense' or 'relaxed'. Performances were presented as audio-only, audio-video, or video-only

Source: Adapted from Li, 2020

kind of visual indication, the applause all performers hope for will be late in coming and more tentative than one would like.

In a non-musical context, the McGurk effect tells us how auditory and visual information are integrated in the perception of spoken syllables: for example, hearing 'ba' but seeing the lip movement of 'ga' generates the impression of 'da'.[2] Similarly, arm and body movements in music performance may influence listeners' perception of emotions, pitch intervals, consonance and dissonance, duration, and musical expressivity (see Schutz, 2008).

Teaching and learning piano timbre cross-modally

In the three weeks' observational study of piano lessons of three pairs of university-level teachers and students, I found frequent use of metaphors, adjectives, gestures, and embodied actions to explain timbral intentions. At times, verbal descriptions of timbral concepts were quite abstract and hard to translate into piano performance, for example, 'men's voices', 'bellringing from a distance', or 'richer' and 'fuller'. While timbre targets can be hard to understand and communicate compared to other performance targets (e.g., dynamics, timing), it seemed that using abstract concepts was made possible through co-construction of concepts by both teachers and students, so by encouraging participation from students. Instead of mere imitation, reference to proprioceptive feelings helped the students to connect their movements to sound, interoceptive feelings, and mental activities. My research findings suggested that language and conversation play an important role in the teaching of timbre among university-level teachers and students as relatively much discussion was held during episodes dealing with timbre (see Vignette 2). Discussion in the context of performance enables timbre to be co-constructed and developed 'in-the-moment' through embodied musical experience that needs active participation from both teacher and student (Li & Timmers, 2021).

In addition, or as part of the discussions of timbre, modelling, metaphors, and descriptions of concrete musical results were frequently used, each of which are briefly summarised below: *Modelling* was widely used in the piano lessons and worked as an auditory presentation to the student. Dickey (1992) regarded modelling as the most effective approach for teaching pupils concepts of timbre: pupils may fail to discriminate between different timbres by just being told of 'rich', 'bright', or 'thin' sounds, and their motoric skills cannot be improved just by discussing the tempo and metre. However, several scholars have also mentioned limitations of modelling, that aural modelling may result in 'mere imitation' (Laukka, 2004). When combined with discussion, many of the disadvantages of modelling can be overcome (see also Chapter 4).

Metaphorical/literal description. Apart from modelling, the teachers gave literal descriptions of musical results (e.g., 'It's getting louder here') to help the student to make sense of musical changes resulting from a timbral effect, hence enabling them to generate an explicit performance plan. Several researchers have mentioned that the use of metaphors, or figurative language, was more effective for students compared to the literal description of playing techniques (Barten, 1998; Schippers, 2006). I have observed a piano teacher instructing her beginner-student in producing a light timbre by using the metaphor of 'imagine the keys are very hot and you are afraid of your fingers being burned' – leading to a remarkably audible improvement in the pupil's performance.

Timbre is relevant to piano teaching and learning at any age

In addition to observing teaching strategies, I asked pianists and the three pairs of teachers-students about their perspectives on teaching and learning of piano timbre. From the interviews with pianists, it was clear that piano timbre was seen as part of lifelong learning. As P1 mentioned, learning of piano timbre 'develops by years and has no pin-point'. Even though they understood the challenges of teaching timbre to young students, as there may be 'no sense of the meaning of timbre' and that they 'couldn't feel the difference' (P4), pianists still stated that teaching of piano timbre should start from a young age rather than 'playing for years' just to 'pass the exams' (P2). The solutions suggested by pianists included building up a 'wider range of repertoire' (P1), 'listening to other pianists' sounds' (P4), and guidance/demonstration by the piano teacher (P3). This suggests that piano teachers may consider teaching piano timbre concepts from early stages.

To facilitate teaching and learning of timbre, pupils can be directed to characteristics related to tone production that are available for reflection and control including touch qualities, the utilisation of weight and energy, and the involvement of different muscle groups. Bodily awareness and sensations are less mentioned and hard to communicate in piano lessons but may benefit from more attention from teachers and students. Each of these points is briefly explained next.

Touch qualities

Finger-key touch is one of the most effective tools enabling pianists to create timbral nuance, other than the pedal. Touch qualities can be classified as attack type (percussive vs non-percussive), size of area contact between fingertips and the keyboard (curved vs straight), duration (legato vs staccato), rigidity (soft vs hard), and the utilisation of different parts of the body (finger-weight vs arm-weight). For example, a small striking surface which uses only the tip of the finger may produce a brilliant, brittle tone; a larger surface using a flatter finger may produce a more ringing and singing tone (Lhévinne, 2013).

Energy, force, and weight

Clearly, when different types of touch are applied to the keyboard, the amount of energy and weight exerted by the body becomes significantly different. Additionally, playing techniques require a pianist to acquire more advanced skills such as considering the direction, flow, and rotation of energy and weight. It is fairly common for pianists to make elegant arm movements even in the production of very light notes or chords. Whilst these large arm movements may not be required to produce light notes, they may nevertheless be used to create a certain sound, as if there is a 'flow' of energy that is transferred from the performer's body to the keyboard and the string of the piano. This might be the reason why musicians in the interviews I conducted described their sounds as moving (the sound 'travels') or having direction (the sound 'moves forward' into the keys) (see Vignette 1).

Tension and relaxation

Muscular relaxation and tension are important variables in piano performance and need to be correctly utilised, combined, and interchanged in the production of piano timbre; even in the full-relaxation approach (Kochevitsky, 1967; Neuhaus, 1993; Hamilton, 2012), there is still some degree of tension in the finger joints. The challenge in piano teaching and learning is not just about understanding the exertion of a performance action from particular joints and muscles; rather, it lies in the extent to which a pupil can learn to control and monitor relaxation, and also the ability to be aware of, and distinguish between, tension and relaxation. My research revealed that vivid metaphors and figurative language can offer effective tools for teachers to help students understand kinaesthetic experiences relating to weight, direction, and tension.

Bodily sensations

Piano playing does not involve solely physical movements; the pianist gets abundant information through interacting with the instrument and from their bodily feelings. Several piano pedagogues have emphasised the importance of being aware of bodily sensations in piano playing. For example, Fielden (1927) emphasised the idea of sensing muscular contraction and suggested that pupils who do not sense muscular contraction when playing should place a hand lightly on a table and then press with enough tension to experience the feeling of muscular contraction. Levinskaya (1930) also suggested that it was imperative for pianists to learn, and be aware of, which lever (i.e., joint) they intended to use and then to create a firm ground for operating this action by fixing some joints with muscular contraction. In this way, bodily awareness – a sense of proprioception – helps the pianist to monitor and improve their playing action. During the teaching observation study, I found that teachers used questions, dialogue, and instructive language effectively to guide students' independent thinking of bodily sensations, which may be difficult to communicate solely through modelling.

To sum up, the teaching and learning of weight, energy, force, relaxation/tension, and proprioceptive feeling in piano playing helps to integrate mind and body. Proprioception closes the feedforward and feedback loop by bringing awareness to bodily sensations and mental content, which in turn can be used to refine future actions and utilisation of weight, energy, and so on. The development of the skills mentioned above takes years of training. In this sense, the teaching and learning of piano timbre can be regarded as a lifelong learning process.

Vignettes

Vignette 1

The following example illustrates pianists' embodied and blended concept of timbre: ways in which abstract timbral intentions are related to and shaped by performative gestures (see Li & Timmers, 2020, for a full discussion). P1 in my interview study explained that:

> This open phrase, it is quite a rich chord to me. It will be under this bit ((the space under the hand)) where to me the sound comes from ((Gesture 1, left panel of Figure 5.2)). However, if it is played with the flatter finger ((Gesture 2, right panel of

Figure 5.2 Hand-gestures illustrating timbral intentions
Source: Adapted from Li, 2020

> Figure 5.2)), to me it sounds a little bit hollow, it is not very *pronounced* enough to start the opening of a phrase.
>
> [emphasis added]

She further mentioned that

> the way you shape your fingers over the keys, that links to how much sound you have under here ((the hand)). If the finger is flat, there is less *room* for you to shape the sound.
>
> [emphasis added]

In this case, the pianist paralleled the shape of hand with the mouth (i.e., finger-key space becomes the symbol of space in the mouth) and associated the touch quality with embodied experience of vocal pronunciation (Figure 5.2).

Vignette 2

The following vignette from a teacher (T) and student (S) in the observational study illustrates how questions, dialogue, and instructing language helped to develop a shared understanding of timbre concepts.

T: Have a listen this time, what do you think is different compared to last time?
S: It's deeper. . . .
T: Hmm. . . . Did it change? What do you think changed?
S: Well, this time I felt the sound was more 'solid' – compared with the last performance – which was 'crisp' – this one was more 'solid, and 'heavier'.

Developing timbre on the piano 57

T: The reason for the so-called heavier sound was because you played heavily. But you should – and maybe you're not – feel the energy flowing from the back of the hand and going through the fingers.
S: Yes, I felt that.

The teacher's questions had a positive influence on the student's independent thinking – the student learnt to discriminate differences in piano timbre and use metaphorical descriptors to express their feeling, including those of 'deeper', 'solid', and 'heavier'. The teacher tried to guide the student to think of the use of energy, to let the student feel differences in timbre by distinguishing 'where the energy comes from'.

Conclusion and implications for practice

This chapter discussed the importance of timbre in the context of music performance and education and draws readers' attention to a wider understanding of the notion of timbre that goes beyond the sonic dimension. Timbre is a concept determined by multiple factors including performance gestures, musical structure, expressive intentions, and psychological and proprioceptive feelings. Bodily movements of performers not only enrich their own experiences of timbre but also influence audiences' musical perception. Given this, music teachers should be aware of the fact that learning of timbre is not only related to motoric skills or aural ability but requires multiple levels of body-mind integration.

When we are persuaded by the idea that timbre is not merely a matter of sound, it makes it easier to apply this knowledge to daily practice. I have encountered many pianists saying that the instruments that are available to them for teaching or practice are of low quality, which discourages them from working on timbre. Indeed, timbral nuances seem like a luxury feature for an electronic piano and a hard requirement for pupils who experience many other learning challenges in note reading, technical coordination, musical interpretation, and expressiveness. Nevertheless, I suggest that learning of timbres should start at the beginning stage of musical training to establish aural sensitivity and mental awareness to timbre, no matter what quality of instruments students practise or learn upon.

The training of mental skills in timbre learning is as important as the development of physical skills. The process of tone production could be regarded as an integration of mind and body that involves the awareness of mental concepts, actions, ears, and sounds. The absence of one of these elements may result in a feeling of 'just playing'.[3] I would suggest that music teachers focus on enhancing awareness to mobilise timbre and cultivate the sensitivity of feeling timbre from the earlier stages of music learning.

One last piece of advice for music teachers and students is about the performance gestures and visual communication in the musical performance. Some performers are already very good at communicating with listeners through sound but could better utilise the additional visual information in their musical communication with audiences. I suggest that musicians embrace the visual impact of their performances, as it adds extra 'flavours' and 'dimensions' to the audience's perceptions of performed sounds. As performers and teachers, we need to be aware of the roles of musical gestures in terms of enriching our own performance experience, enhancing the musical expressivity and the communication with audiences.

Main points

- Timbre is not only a matter of sound.
- Timbre can be perceived both aurally and visually.
- Visual information helps performers to communicate timbre intentions.
- Verbal descriptions of timbre are linked with psychological and bodily experiences.
- Teaching and learning of piano timbre is a lifelong process that extends beyond technique development but integrates body and mind.
- Teachers are advised to start the cultivation of the conception of piano timbre at early stages of piano learning.

Notes

1 Proprioception is a specific type of interoception (proprietary meaning 'one's own'). 'Proprioception gathers information about pressure and temperature from the skin receptors, the relative state of the body segments, balance and posture, skin-stretch, fatigue, and effort as well as information from internal organs' (Eilan, Marcel, & Bermúdez, 1995, p. 12).
2 Illustration of McGurk effect: www.youtube.com/watch?v=jtsfidRq2tw
3 'Just playing' normally refers to non (or less) expressive performance. In the context of timbre production, 'just playing' refers to the lack of bodily awareness, which is in contrast with the state of 'mindfulness' in musical performance.

References

American National Standards Institute. (1973). *American National Standard Institute: Psychoacoustical terminology* (Timbre. ANSI S3.20 1973) (p. 56). Author.

Barten, S. S. (1998). Speaking of music: The use of motor-affective metaphors in music instruction. *Journal of Aesthetic Education*, *32*(2), 89–97. https://doi.org/10.2307/3333561

Dickey, M. R. (1992). A review of research on modeling in music teaching and learning. *Bulletin of the Council for Research in Music Education*, *113*, 27–40.

Doğantan-Dack, M. (2011). In the beginning was gesture: Piano touch and the phenomenology of the performing body. In A. Gritten & E. King (Eds.), *New perspectives on music and gesture* (pp. 243–265). Ashgate.

Eilan, N., Marcel, A., & Bermúdez, J.-L. (1995). Self-consciousness and the body. In J.-L. Bermúdez, A. Marcel, & N. Eilan (Eds.), *The body and the self* (pp. 1–28). MIT Press.

Fielden, T. (1927). *The science of pianoforte technique*. Macmillan.

Goebl, W., Bresin, R., & Fujinaga, I. (2014). Perception of touch quality in piano tones. *The Journal of the Acoustical Society of America*, *136*(5), 2839–2850. https://doi.org/10.1121/1.4896461

Hamilton, C. G. (2012). *Touch and expression in piano playing*. Dover Publication, Inc.

Kochevitsky, G. (1967). *The art of piano playing: A scientific approach*. Summy-Birchard Music.

Laukka, P. (2004). Instrumental music teachers' views on expressivity: A report from music conservatoires. *Music Education Research*, *6*(1), 45–56. https://doi.org/10.1080/1461380032000182821

Levinskaya, M. (1930). *The Levinskaya System of pianoforte technique and tone-colour through mental and muscular control*. J. M. Dent and Sons, Ltd.

Lhévinne, J. (2013). *Basic principles in pianoforte playing*. Courier Corporation.

Li, S. (2020). *An embodied perspective on piano timbre: Conceptualisation and communication in performance and educational context* [Doctoral thesis, The University of Sheffield]. http://etheses.whiterose.ac.uk/27976/

Li, S., & Timmers, R. (2020). Exploring pianists' embodied concepts of piano timbre: An interview study. *Journal of New Music Research*, *49*(5), 477–492. https://doi.org/10.1080/09298215.2020.1826532

Li, S., & Timmers, R. (2021). Mind-body integration and teacher-student interaction in the teaching and learning of piano timbre in lessons. *Frontiers in Psychology*, *12*, 1671.

Neuhaus, H. (1993). *The art of piano playing*. London: Kahn & Averill.

Ortmann, O. (1925). *The physical basis of piano touch and tone*. E.P. Dutton.

Parncutt, R., & Troup, M. (2002). Piano. In R. Parncutt & G. McPherson (Eds.), *The science and psychology of music performance: Creative strategies for teaching and learning* (pp. 285–302). Oxford University Press.

Rosen, C. (2002). *Piano notes: The world of the pianist*. Simon and Schuster.

Schippers, H. (2006). 'As if a little bird is sitting on your finger. . .': Metaphor as a key instrument in training professional musicians. *International Journal of Music Education*, *24*(3), 209–217. https://doi.org/10.1177/0255761406069640

Schutz, M. (2008). Seeing music? What musicians need to know about vision. *Empirical Musicology Review*, *3*(3), 83–108. https://doi.org/10.18061/1811/34098

Traube, C. (2004). *An interdisciplinary study of the timbre of the classical guitar* [Unpublished doctoral dissertation, McGill University].

Turner, E. O. (1939). Touch and tone-quality: The pianist's illusion. *The Musical Times*, *80*(1153), 173–176. https://doi.org/10.2307/921167

6 Mobilising improvisation skills in classically trained musicians

Jonathan Ayerst

Introduction

I realise now, looking back on a fairly long career as a professional performing musician, that I always wanted to improvise. The desire to create my own music, to be more at one with the sounds I made, faded into the background as I embarked on an intensive musical training as a solo pianist and absorbed the culture and practice of European classical music. For many years I thought of improvisation as something which existed 'out there' but it was something which other people did – jazz musicians, avant-garde composers, legendary geniuses such as Beethoven or Mozart. Later, when I started working with a contemporary music group I often needed to improvise in a modern, atonal language based on the composers' written instructions. My old desire to improvise resurfaced as I felt quite comfortable with this style, but when I tried to extend this positive experience to improvising on more classical, tonal models of repertoire my confidence faltered: although I could imagine the music I wanted to improvise, as soon as I sat down at the instrument, nothing seemed to work. My fingers did not respond well to my musical ideas, the results sounded poor, and I felt so uncomfortable that I soon gave up.

Summary of the research

Such was the background to my PhD, an autoethnographic study through which I learnt to become fluent in improvising on Baroque models of organ repertoire, while at the same time documenting the learning process in written, audio, and visual recordings. The data that emerged from these records I compared with a wide range of written literature in cognitive psychology, improvisation treatises, and other autoethnographic studies of learning to perform; and this research model allowed me to reflect on my experience and to understand better the emotional and cognitive barriers I needed to overcome, and, after a while, the learning experience as a whole. As I began the study, I framed my research questions in the following way:

1 Why was I, a trained and experienced musician, unable to improvise? Why didn't my existing knowledge in interpreting scores and my instrumental technique allow me to improvise?
2 Why did I feel so embarrassed about improvising? Why was I so critical of my own music?
3 What kind of specialised knowledge do expert improvisers possess? How could I acquire this knowledge? How is this knowledge defined in existing psychological research and theory?
4 What would be the implications of my learning experience for other classical performers and for their teachers?

My position as a researcher gave me the opportunity to examine my thoughts while improvising. This helped me to identify several reasons why initiating the learning process seemed difficult to me, reasons which correspond closely to Hill's (2017) more general findings about the lack of improvisation among classically trained musicians. Briefly summarised, these are: (1) Values: that is, culturally shared beliefs about how music is created and who is entitled to create it, which produced in me a sense of wrong-doing when I tried to improvise. (2) Career Pressures: the self-conscious feeling that, if anyone overheard my improvising, I would receive 'negative feedback for anything that might deviate from the notated score and conventional interpretation' (p. 236), and (3) Education: the realisation that I lacked relevant or specialised skills to draw on when improvising.

Values, self-beliefs, and emotions

My first step toward a better understanding of these problems was to look more carefully at the surrounding musical culture in which I had been trained, a culture which I now perceived as unique in producing several generations of non-improvising musicians (Sawyer, 2008; Moore, 1992). Many texts refer to gradual changes in aesthetical beliefs governing art and music which, toward the end of the 18th century, culminate in what the art historian Gombrich (1964) describes as a new distinction 'between Art with a capital A and the mere exercise of a craft' (p. 377). Writing more specifically about classical music,

Goehr (1994) traces a similar delineation between ad hoc or everyday creativity (i.e., improvisation) and the creative act of serious Art music. Musical practice is described as evolving from a mixed-skill approach in which performance, composition, and improvisation were equally employed, to a more divided system of labour in which creative work was increasingly left to composers whose finished, completed scores were performed by equally specialist interpreters. Pedagogic methods within the new music conservatoires of the 19th century supported this view by training musicians toward ideals of accuracy and the pursuit of technical perfection; to study music became, by default, the service of an interpretation of canonic works. These ideals and beliefs are epitomised in what Goehr describes as attitudes of *Werktreue* toward the printed score (Goehr, 1994).

Identifying such attitudes of *Werktreue* in my own thinking I was able to come to the following conclusions: (1) I thought of music as something which was created by other people, usually historical figures portrayed as 'creative geniuses'. (2) I thought of music in terms of scores rather than in terms of creative processes or musical decisions. (3) I assumed that every note in a musical piece was 'put there for a reason' (Goehr, 1994, p. 172) because my habitual objective as a performer had been to accurately realise every one of these notes; I therefore treated errors as serious failings when I improvised.

Improvising in the classical style

Because of this rooted perception that music was created through mysterious processes, and particularly through my sensitivity to errors, the ad hoc actions of improvising were initially hard to perform. I usually tried to work out every note, hesitating before committing myself to any action which might sound stupid, and this resulted in a cautious, halting way of improvising. I found it impossible to let go and simply play wrong-sounding music, or music which I could not control. Yet, listening to the results I wondered if I were going about learning in the right way: should I not be more willing to experiment, to make mistakes and learn from those mistakes? While I was worrying over every detail, was I not neglecting other skills I had observed in experts: their ability to improvise fluently and without hesitation, their seeming readiness to follow their imagination, to respond quickly to events and to control complete musical structures and forms? These questions arise frequently in discussions about learning to improvise: Hickey (2009), for example, suggests that students should 'develop an improvisatory *disposition*' (p. 292) before trying to acquire craft-like skills or model their work to a particular historic style. Jaques-Dalcroze (1921) also devised his system of eurythmics and aural response, as a method of developing 'that *ensemble* of reactions, impulses, pauses, recoils, and movements' (p. 5) before any theoretical or analytical knowledge was used to control musical improvisation. As for myself, I found I was unwilling to completely abandon my conscious controlled approach, but instead, started to divide my sessions between free and controlled. In this way, I kept most of my improvising within a consciously constructed style but also started to experience another side to improvising which was more fluent, spontaneous, and led by physical sensations rather than controlled calculation.

For me, issues of freedom vs control and the problems of letting go arose more strongly when I improvised using diatonic harmony and/or tried to imitate baroque-style forms such as Preludes and Fugues. If, on the contrary, I improvised in a free, atonal style, or adopted a pentatonic or modal scale-system as a basis for harmonic construction, then the need to organise my thoughts was much less acute. A particular issue in my learning was to discover a balance between freedom of imagination and fluency of action while remaining faithful to a particular historical style. I eventually found this freedom through focusing more systematically on the underlying rules of this music. Particularly useful were Joseph Fux's (1725/1971) rules for the construction of consonant and dissonant intervals in diatonic music,[1] and after I spent some time applying these to my more controlled improvisation sessions (carefully constructing two-voice duets and noticing which intervals were consonant and which dissonant according to the rules), I found I was able to overcome my tendency to hesitate through the surety of the rules. So, while this work was admittedly very slow, I did not find it frustrating because the rules allowed me to improvise without doubt or hesitation – that is, to assemble 'a basic vocabulary' in which 'fundamental perceptual distinctions' could be drawn, offering a clear 'framework for feedback' as Kingscott and Durrant (2010, p. 140) propose. Once these basic rules became assimilated into my playing, I found I could improvise larger sections of music, and thus began to steer my improvising toward the stylistic features of the historical idiom I had chosen. In this way, my learning path followed theoretical models such as Kenny and Gellrich (2002) which describe first acquiring a *hardware* of 'patterns, [. . .] voicings, and counterpoint' on which a stylistic *software* can be constructed of 'melodies, phrases, and larger musical ideas' (p. 130).

Improvisation skills 65

Autoethnographic records and journals

As this was an autoethnographic study of learning to improvise, I needed to keep systematic records as data of my experience. This exercise of regular data collection became an invaluable learning tool, in particular the use of an improvisation logbook in which I wrote down my objectives for each session, possible strategies for obtaining these, and reflections on how each session had gone. The act of writing enabled me to see a different side to my work, one which balanced the impressions I had in the moment of improvising (when my judgement of events tended to be negatively influenced by errors) with a more positive assessment of my progress, for example: 'It takes a while to get going, but with time I always find a solution'. Thus, my written records provided me with a 'go to' place where I could not only reflect upon the experience of improvising more objectively, but also learn to focus more on the learning process than the musical results of my improvising. Later, I extended these written records to drawings and graphic scores (Figure 6.1) which helped me to clarify my mental representation of musical events and eventually to construct larger musical sections.

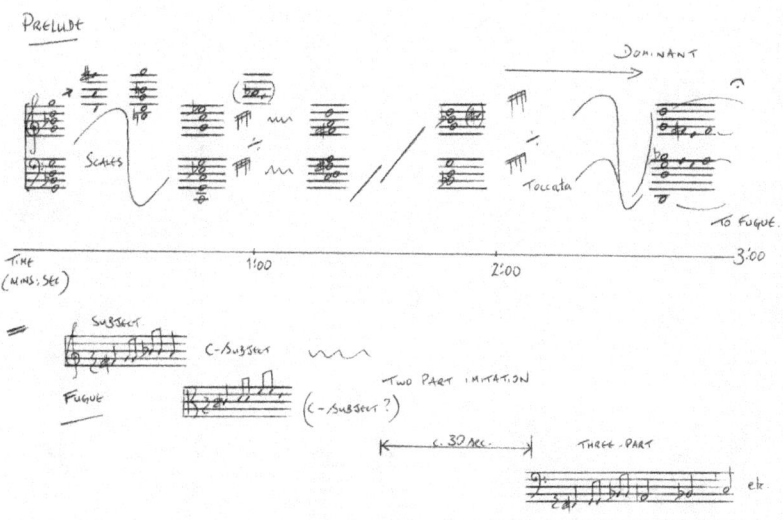

Figure 6.1 Graphic design for an improvised Prelude and Fugue

Attention and decision making

Having now becoming fluent in constructing general, baroque-style musical textures, I still struggled to organise my improvising toward complete musical forms. As a result I often took certain compositions which I liked and used them as models for improvising, analysing all the musical features on which I could possibly improvise: chord progressions, cadences, polyphonic textures, and structural devices such as imitation, melodies, embellishments, accompaniments, and so on. My problem now was which features to select and how to organise them in an expressive, coherent, or formal structure. I was not used to thinking of music in terms of decisions about *what* to play, and therefore I lacked the skills through which to prioritise one feature over another. Looking back, I realise that what now occurred was a conversion of my existing musical knowledge; a fundamental shift from my perspective as interpretive performer (a perspective in which every element in the musical structure is preordained) to agentic creator (who understands that many different realisations of a musical idea are possible, and that musical 'products' are formed as much through decisions taken in a moment as through processes of lengthy reflection). This change of perspective emerged through my continuing analyses of compositional models, in particular as I extended this work to draw up new scores in which only one or two original features were kept. These new scores I used as templates for guiding my improvising (Figure 6.2).

Figure 6.2 The opening bars of the third movement of Trio Sonata BWV 525 for organ, by J. S. Bach (1685–1750), over my own harmonic and rhythmic reductions which functioned as templates for improvisation

Source: Ayerst, 2021

Acquiring a different kind of knowledge

The score extracts in Figure 7.2 are representative of a number of experimental templates which I made for bringing my improvisation closer to a particular musical structure. Each template represented a different element of the score (harmonic, rhythmic, melodic, etc.,) and allowed me to retain something of the original model, while also improvising new material. I was now creating many new versions of the original model: for example, a cadence (bars 4–5) could occur with different voicings, more or less decoration and so on; what was important was that the underlying principle of the *cadence* occurred at that point in the musical narrative. Similarly, the opening sequence of harmonies through which the composer establishes a particular tonality (in this case E-flat major) might be performed using different figurations, different melodies, rhetorical gestures, etc. Again, what remained unchanged was the underlying principle of *establishing a key or tonality*. In this way, through taking a score apart and reconstructing it in different ways, my perception of the music seemed to go behind the finished surface of the score to find an underlying structure of functional-expressive principles which could be realised in many different ways. These underlying principles I represented to myself as abstract concepts: *opening moves, introduction of a second voice, sequence to provide interlude, partial return to tonic*, and so on.

As I began to perceive music in terms of underlying concepts which could be realised in numerous ways, so did I make a significant leap forwards as an improviser. Instead of feeling overwhelmed by the need to control every note in the musical texture, I now selected features and improvised on them more freely. At first, I improvised quite simple music using just one feature at a time; later, I learnt to combine features in a way which made the music more interesting, and which brought my improvisations closer to the composed model. Using these features in a general way I found a balance between the constraints of the stylistic model and the freedom of my own imagination. This is not to say that I had yet found my own creative voice as an improviser; rather, I was learning to improvise within a certain historic style, to overcome hesitation and gain fluency within this style. Although working in this way was slow and involved a great deal of conscious calculation, I found it rewarding because I was gaining expressive control over my improvising. As I continued to analyse and combine different features of an increasing range of models my ability to select and mentally represent such features become more refined. In addition, I found that, by reducing the improvising to a simple framework, I created pathways to more complex, fluent actions: for increasingly short sequences of rapid and unconscious movements emerged as embellishments and variations of the simple principles I was focusing on. These movements were usually performed before I could be aware of them and were my first experience of 'real' improvising – that is, stylistic yet intuitive improvising, linked directly to my imagination rather than effortful, conscious control.

Conclusion and implications for practice

My training as an interpretive performer in European classical music did not provide me with the skills I needed for improvising. When I tried, I felt embarrassed about creating my own music and self-critical of the results. Keeping a written journal of each improvisation session helped me to plan strategies and to reflect objectively on my progress; also, it taught me to focus more upon the events of learning, rather than the musical results.

As an interpretive performer I was used to caring about every detail of the musical texture. As I started to improvise this perspective changed and I thought of musical structure as a fluid construction – the result of musical decisions which could render structural principles in many different ways. Selecting individual features of the musical texture on which to improvise and reducing complex structures to simple principles allowed me to develop my own musical decision making toward expressive ends.[2]

Improvising my own versions of written compositions made me feel closer to that music, as if I could share the composer's perspective of events. I gained my most valuable insights not from written treatises or following prescribed methods, but by inventing my own exercises and learning strategies. Gaining control over my learning in this way also helped me to feel a valuable sense of agency as an improviser, through which I was more willing to act and to follow my imagination without hesitation.

The challenge of general pedagogic strategies for improvisation

Traditional methods of pedagogy (e.g., Dupré, 1925; Schouten, 1955) have tended to revolve around the expertise of a single individual which is codified into a particular approach or a series of exercises. However, alongside other researchers, I question the usefulness of such methods which (1) assume a particular musical style is suitable for all students of improvisation (Hickey, 2009), or (2) that valuable insights (such as the changes in perception of musical structure I have described) will be communicated merely through 'presenting' rules and exercises (Berkowitz, 2010). Nevertheless, useful insights can be drawn from my experience of learning to improvise which can add to the ongoing debate concerning pedagogical methods. For example, my use of rules and constraints to gain clarity in thinking, to better organise my actions, and to align my improvising with a particular style seemingly disagrees with the notion that rules can inhibit creativity and imagination (e.g., Dolan, 2005). Yet it is important to note the way in which I acquired these rules and appropriated them as solutions to problems which gradually emerged during several months of free experimentation. Rather than learning through externally applied rules, I devised my own rules internally, through processes of analysing compositional models, adapting existing theories (such as Fux's [1725/1971] rules of intervallic motion) and constructing my own exercises. Thus, I used rules more as a helpful guide to better orientate my improvisation and organise my thoughts, rather than as an imposed system of abstract constraints.

The advantage of an autoethnographic account is that it emphasises the student's perspective throughout the learning process, a perspective which may be significantly different from the expert's. Understanding a learner's priorities, their focus of attention, their 'flow of control' (Anderson, 1982) over the task helps to construct a more flexible, individual approach to learning which might begin with an investigation of a student's reasons for improvising. Adopting such a flexible approach to teaching improvisation implies a departure from purely instructional models of teaching. Borgo (2007), for example, suggests that 'the notion of teachers as "experts" and "gatekeepers" must ultimately give way to the more engaged and interactive role of mentors and facilitators' (p. 69), a viewpoint echoed by other studies (i.e., Hickey, 2009). During my own studies I also observed many improvisation lessons at secondary and tertiary level in which I noticed students responding more positively to teachers who shared their position as learners, were willing to experiment alongside them and allowed themselves to make mistakes. Demonstrations of expertise often seemed to demotivate the student, and I often overheard comments such as 'I will never be able to play like that!'

It is worth noting that a permissive use of language, such as 'Did you know that you can . . . ?' and 'I found out that you can . . .' (Knight, 2009 p. 74) is particularly effective in facilitating the learner's sense of freedom and readiness to experiment, especially when modelling improvisation on a particular style or constraints, while the more coercive 'You should . . .' or 'You have to . . .' can generate a sense of helplessness as to how to respond. Therefore, in many cases the first pedagogical step is simply to create a context where the student feels safe to improvise without fear of critical feedback (Custodero, 2007). While I was learning to improvise, I had the opportunity to compare my own learning experience with my two sons (aged six and ten) who started piano lessons and were improvising freely at the piano without any fear of critical feedback or self-consciousness. In their case, mobilising their improvisation skills involved simply allowing them to explore the instrument and the music they were learning without stopping them!

Looking back, the most important things I learnt about improvising came from the actual experience of doing, and for this reason I urge all would-be improvisers to engage in the task, to *mobilise* their own improvisational skills. Although my learning path can be seen to correspond to general theories of skill learning (e.g., Schneider & Fisk, 1982) in that what was first effortful and calculated became gradually automatic and fluent, I did not learn by trying to follow a theoretically prescribed path. Instead, my learning came from first trying in a general way to improvise and then progressively taking more control over the process, for example by devising strategies such as writing out score templates which focused my attention in a more productive way. *Mobilising* my improvising in this way led me to see 'behind the score' to the constructive principles on which the music was built.

In summary I return to my opening research question concerning what kind of *knowledge* I gained which I now use to improvise. This knowledge I would divide into three parts: (1) theoretical – the rules, conscious strategies, written exercises and research I use to improvise; (2) embodied – my physical sensations, the coordination between my fingers and imagination, my intuitive responses which emerge in the moment of improvising; and (3) agentic – involving my readiness to take ownership of the music, to take musical decisions without hesitation, and communicate expressively through improvising.

Main points

- Cultural ideals in European classical music practice can affect the view of oneself as a creative agent and need to be actively addressed.
- New tasks can quickly become overwhelming and demotivating. Selecting features of musical texture and improvising on each feature in turn can help to organise thoughts and actions.

- Taking agency over one's learning and deliberately driving change may be best achieved by inventing one's own improvisation exercises.
- A flexible, open-ended approach to teaching improvisation is more valuable than any one pedagogical method. Expertise is not a prerequisite for teaching improvisation, though experience is useful.
- There is much existing research into improvisation which helps to inform the learning process. Ultimately though, essential knowledge is gained only through action – 'just doing it', and through mobilising one's own improvising skills.

Notes

1 Fux intended these rules as a basis to the construction of Renaissance-style counterpoint, epitomised by Palestrina, but they function excellently as rules for constructing diatonic harmony.
2 Fulara (2013) names 15 different elements on which one can improvise: 'rhythm (the lengths of subsequent notes and pauses), time (the situation of sounds against the metronomic points), meter, tempo, melics, melodics (the location of the heights of the sounds, sonic material, scales), dynamics (changes in the intensity of sound), articulation (the way of extracting the sound for groups of sounds and or a single sound), harmony (chord consonance), colour (timbre), phrasing, form, accentuating (connected with rhythm, dynamics and phrasing), agogics (as the proportion of the amount of notes to the tempo of the piece), texture, interpretation (the way of operating and connecting elements of music by the performer' (p. 423).

References

Anderson, J. (1982). Acquisition of cognitive skill. *Psychological Review, 89*(4), 369–406. https://doi.org/10.1037/0033-295X.89.4.369

Berkowitz, A. (2010). *The improvising mind: Cognition and creativity in the musical moment.* Oxford University Press.

Borgo, D. (2007). Free jazz in the classroom: An ecological approach to music education. *Jazz Perspectives, 1*(1), 61–88. https://doi.org/10.1080/17494060601061030

Custodero, L. (2007). Origins and expertise in the improvisation of adults and children: A phenomenological study of content and process. *British Journal of Music Education, 24*(1), 77–98. https://doi.org/10.1017/S0265051706007236

Dolan, D. (2005). Back to the future: Towards the revival of extemporisation in classical music performance. In G. Odam & N. Bannan (Eds.), *The reflective conservatoire: Studies in music education* (pp. 97–136). Ashgate Publishing Ltd.

Dupré, M. (1925). *Cours complet d'improvisation à l'orgue.* Alphonse Leduc.
Fulara, A. (2013). The model of counterpoint improvisation and the methods of improvisation in popular music. *Avant: Trends in Interdisciplinary Studies,* 4(1), 417–454. https://doi.org/10.12849/40102013.0106.0022
Fux, J. J. (1971). *The study of counterpoint* (A. Mann, Trans., J. Edmunds, Ed.). W.W. Norton. (Original work published in 1725)
Goehr, L. (1994). *The imaginary museum of musical works: An essay in the philosophy of music.* Clarendon Press.
Gombrich, E. H. (1964). *The story of art.* The Phaidon Press.
Hickey, M. (2009). Can improvisation be 'taught'?: A call for free improvisation in our schools. *International Journal of Music Education,* 27(4), 285–299. https://doi.org/10.1177/0255761409345442
Hill, J. (2017). Incorporating improvisation into classical music performance. In J. Rink, H. Gaunt, & A. Williamon (Eds.), *Musicians in the making: Pathways to creative performance.* Oxford University Press.
Jaques-Dalcroze, E. (1921). *Rhythm, music and education.* Chatto & Windus.
Kenny, B., & Gellrich, M. (2002). Improvisation. In R. Parncutt & G. McPherson (Eds.), *The science and psychology of music performance: Creative strategies for teaching and learning* (pp. 116–134). Oxford University Press.
Kingscott, J., & Durrant, C. (2010). Keyboard improvisation: A phenomenological study. *International Journal of Music Education,* 28(2), 127–144. https://doi.org/10.1177/0255761410362941
Knight, P. (2009). Creativity and improvisation: A journey into music. In B. L. Bartleet, & C. Ellis (Eds.), *Music autoethnographies: Making autoethnography sing/making music personal* (pp. 73–84). Australian Academic Press.
Moore, R. (1992). The decline of improvisation in western art music: An interpretation of change. *International Review of the Aesthetics and Sociology of Music,* 23(1), 61–84. https://doi.org/10.2307/836956
Sawyer, R. K. (2008). Learning music from collaboration. *International Journal of Educational Research,* 47(1), 50–59. https://doi.org/10.1016/j.ijer.2007.11.004
Schneider, W., & Fisk, A. D. (1982). Attention theory and mechanisms for skilled performance. *Memory and Control of Action, Advances in Psychology,* 12, 119–143. https://doi.org/10.1016/S0166-4115(08)61989-5
Schouten, H. (1955). *Improvisation on the organ* (J. L. Warren, Trans.). W. Paxton & Co.

Part III
Group leadership and interaction in ensembles

7 Communication and interaction in ensemble rehearsal

Nicola Pennill

Introduction

My interest in ensemble communication and interaction arose from both a love of ensemble playing, and a professional interest in how effective teams form and develop. Working in many kinds of organisations, I became intrigued by the ways in which teams change over time, what constitutes high levels of team performance, and how these concepts might apply in the special setting of the music ensemble. For example, in the Western classical tradition, members of ensembles prepare for performance in various ways. They may practise individual parts, listen to recordings, explore background to repertoire, and plan concerts and rehearsal dates. For most, however, the main way that progress is made is when the group gets together in the rehearsal room and starts to make music together. It is in these times together that the future performance is most clearly imagined, conceived, and brought to life. There are many processes involved, from the refinement of musical sounds to the discussion of possible interpretations. Every group will have unique challenges and strengths, and it is partly for this reason that the process of rehearsal cannot be reduced to a formula, or to a precise set of steps to be executed. Yet there are some common features, and it is those which formed the starting point for this research.

Firstly, rehearsal involves people, interacting with each other. Whilst this might sound obvious, its significance may be under-estimated by those who believe that success lies solely in the quality of musical and technical contributions. It may be insufficiently addressed, as social interaction may be seen as a given, or too sensitive to be worked on explicitly. Secondly, rehearsal evolves over time. This is important because depending on what stage a group is at in their preparation, whether in a single rehearsal or a series, there may be differences in how decisions and progress are made.

DOI: 10.4324/9781003108382-10

So, what does this mean in practice? And given these assumptions, how can members of ensembles harness and use knowledge about interactions and developments over time to maximise their chances of successful performance? The research described in this chapter seeks to answer these questions, at least in part, by offering insights into the development of communication and interaction in the context of small ensembles in rehearsal.

Summary of the research

Whilst it has its own unique context, a musical ensemble has much in common with other types of work groups. For example, small ensembles can be regarded as a type of 'self-managed' team (Gilboa & Tal-Shmotkin, 2012), which has characteristics in common with 'expert' teams where members are highly specialised and skilled (Ericsson et al., 2018), or even with 'swift-starting' action teams, such as emergency response teams, who may not have worked together before (McKinney, Barker, et al., 2005). Ensembles have also been compared to types of sports teams, where the ability to perform under pressure is essential (Fiore & Salas, 2006). Drawing such comparisons can be valuable to highlight aspects of ensemble performance, such as nonverbal communication, which may not be directly related to music making but are nonetheless key to success.

Small musical groups – the particular focus of this chapter – have significant agency over their outcomes. Unlike a large group where a conductor is a major focus of attention and direction, in a small group multiple modes of communication are used by all members. Schütz (1951) described the process of coming together with others to create music as a process of 'mutual tuning-in', in which existing knowledge and predefined 'rules' also shape expectations and outcomes. These 'tuning-in' processes are particularly key in rehearsal, especially where musical relationships are being formed or re-established. One of the goals is to establish a performance which, at least in the Western classical tradition, is generally nonverbal; the time for discussion has passed, and communication has become aural, nonverbal, and implicit. But how does this happen in practice? Is it gradual, or sudden? What is different from the first rehearsal to final run through? What changes, when and how?

Previous research has explored aspects of communication and interaction, and the respective contributions of verbal and nonverbal communication in small ensembles. Davidson and Good (2002) were among the first to deliberately separate the socio-cultural from the musical aspects of a rehearsing ensemble, and to highlight their inter-relationships. In a case study of a student string quartet they identified distinct roles, and different modes of communication used to deal with issues as they arose, such as problems with tuning, or musical timing. Verbal communication related to both social or musical content, and nonverbal communication was a complex mix of gestures, body movements, and eye contact at key moments. Seddon and Biasutti (2009) used case studies of a string quartet and a jazz sextet to explore communication, and categorised verbal and nonverbal communication as instructional, co-operational, and collaborative.

Whilst it is well accepted that there is a time-based dimension to preparing ensemble performance, most studies of ensemble communication have investigated a single rehearsal or a very short time period. Among the relatively few who considered longer time scales, Kokotsaki (2007) found differences between newly formed and established groups, in which the latter were better able to manage time constraints by balancing personal preparation with time in the rehearsal room. This evolving capability was an example of what she described as a more integrated state, in which a 'group kind of self' (p. 658) emerged from collective efforts, and in which individual contributions were subsumed to the overall musical result. Related to this, the transformation from rehearsal to performance in the ensemble has been explained by a shift in the types of exchange between members from 'communication' (which is explicit, such as verbal exchange) to 'interaction' (generally implicit and nonverbal) as performance approaches (King & Gritten, 2017). Also driving this change is the increasing scarcity of time, and the need to embed nonverbal communication required for performance.

To explore further how these elements of time and communication are organised in small ensembles, my research adopted a longitudinal case study approach to see how two newly formed ensembles developed toward a first performance. Working with two small vocal ensembles over roughly a three-month period, I investigated the groups' interpersonal interactions, and how these were shaped in a series of rehearsals (Pennill, 2019). Each ensemble comprised five advanced *a cappella* singers; Group 1 prepared from scratch for a performance in Week 9 of the study, and Group 2 for a performance in Week 16. In the first part of the study the discussions which took place during rehearsal were transcribed and coded using the 'Behaviour in Teams' scheme (Farley et al., 2018), and then analysed for patterns over time using the software THEME (Magnusson, 2000).

In the second part of the study, singers were interviewed three months after the first rehearsal. In order to draw out individual experiences, ensemble members were asked to reflect on the overall process of working together, from first rehearsal to performance. Each was invited to draw a timeline of key events and milestones and describe their experiences and impact of events on the group's progression (Bischof et al., 2011). Emergent themes were identified from the interview accounts and timelines and grouped into activities according to their sequence.

The main findings were that: (1) There were distinct phases of focused development linked by rapid transitions, rather than steady, linear progress. The transitions were triggered by shifts in group dynamics, time constraints, and external events. (2) Communication between group members changed in frequency and character over time, with more nonverbal communication later in the period of study. These two main findings will be considered in turn and discussed in relation to the implications for ensemble interaction and communication.

Phases and transitions of development

The findings from the interviews and drawings revealed similarities between groups in their overall trajectory of development. There were also key events which appeared to act as 'triggers' to subsequent development and catalysts for change and acting as turning points (see Vignette 1 for examples of these). These events provided a renewed sense of resolve and urgency, or a perception of increased convergence around shared ideas and goals. Three main groups of activities emerged according to an approximate time-based sequence. These groups, characterised as 'phases', comprised an initial orientation period, a more volatile and turbulent phase, and a culminating period of coming together as performance approached. These phases are further summarised as follows:

- Phase 1 'Exploration': early processes of orientation, familiarisation with co-performers and goals, establishing communication, and trying out new ideas.
- Phase 2 'Transition': in which there was more conflict, disruption, openness to external influences, and emotional volatility.
- Phase 3 'Integration': the emergence of mutual trust, more direct communication, more efficient ways of working, and growth.

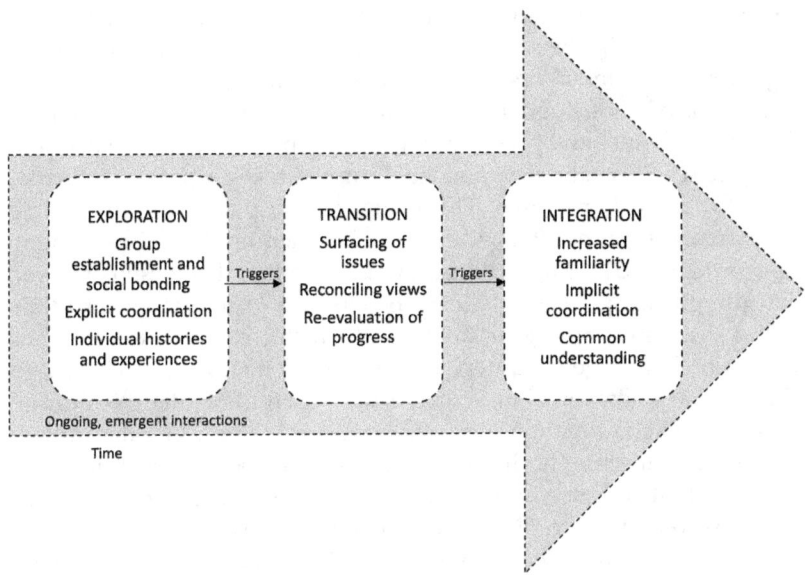

Figure 7.1 A dynamic model of performance preparation
Source: Pennill, 2019

Figure 7.1 summarises the main behaviours that were observed over time, in relation to the phases identified.

Verbal and nonverbal communication

Alongside the phases, there was evidence of a shift from verbal to nonverbal communication over the course of performance preparation, with less time spent talking and more time spent singing. There were also changes observed in the patterns of interaction which were detected using the THEME software. The verbal interaction patterns revealed changes in the complexity of patterns, as indicated by the number of interactions, their length, and the number of ensemble members interacting. Notably, there were peaks of complexity of interaction at the midway point (which was in Week 5 for Group 1, Week 8 for Group 2). These peaks of activity reflected the fact that more group members were contributing to the discussion around more diverse topics, as the group members proposed and tried out ideas, and explored effective ways to work together. As performance approached, however, there was a need to move toward more predictable interactions and for more nonverbal communication to predominate. Accordingly, there was a reduction in the number and length of verbal exchanges involving fewer group members in later weeks of rehearsal.

The episodes of singing also became longer, as the groups refined their programmes and presentation. In Group 2, a detailed analysis was conducted of how the group tackled tuning, a key aspect of rehearsal focus for a vocal ensemble. This study tracked pitch drift and tuning consistency over time, along with verbal interactions and rehearsal strategies relating to tuning (D'Amario et al., 2018). The results showed that the group spent a significant proportion of their rehearsal time (32%) discussing tuning in Week 1, which decreased to 8% in Week 16, in which a range of strategies were discussed and tried. This example illustrates how verbal interactions were used to highlight issues and strategies which were then successfully embedded nonverbally, through singing. In this case, having not sung together before, each member brought their unique vocal qualities, pre-existing knowledge, and the skills involved in controlling their respective voices.

In summary, this research combined observation of interactive behaviours with accounts from the lived experience of members of these small groups. It served to highlight common factors shared by both groups, including the phases of development and changes in communication type, within a context which for each ensemble is unique and constantly changing.

Vignettes

Vignette 1: key events in a group's development can shape progress

Through the personal accounts of the group's development 'stories', common elements emerged around key events and turning points. Group 1 members described how their early rehearsals were focused on getting to know each other, and sight reading lots of new repertoire. There was then a 'reality check' moment when choices of repertoire needed to be made, performances did not go well enough, or illness interfered with rehearsal plans. At this point there was a more concerted effort to focus, or as one member described it:

> . . . it took a while to get going, we coasted a bit, and then we realised we didn't have very long to prepare!
>
> (Bass, Group 1)

There were also some differences of opinion, ascribed to time pressures and lack of focus:

> ... because we were on a very tight schedule for getting the music ready ... then we were like, OK, we've got to start. Yeah, we've got to seriously get on with it
>
> (Tenor, Group 1).

Finally, there was rising confidence and a sense of shared achievement, as the performance goals seemed more attainable. The soprano saw this as a turning point, where

> ... we decided we could do a really good job, so we put everything into it.
>
> (Soprano, Group 1)

They also had a professional coaching session, which provided an additional confidence boost and motivation, enabling them to make further performance refinements. These milestones are shown in Figure 7.1, and in relation to the phases of performance (see Phases and transitions of development).

Taking an overview of the whole experience, the bass described the process in terms of group development and creative growth, moving from 'everyone singing the way they were used to', then being exposed to new ideas and being eager for input, and finally having the confidence as group to weigh alternatives and take more artistic risks:

> I see it as having been in three phases. So, as I say, we started at the start of the year we know you had everyone singing in the way they were totally used to ... and I think there was a period around halfway through the term where we were just like very eager for instruction and a still a little reticent ... and [now] I think the trend is that ... we are a bit maybe a bit more daring ... and saying dare we do this, how does that sound? And previously we would have dismissed it out of hand or not considered it.
>
> (Bass, Group 1)

Key events from both groups, and how they relate to the three phases identified are summarised in Figure 7.2.

82 *Nicola Pennill*

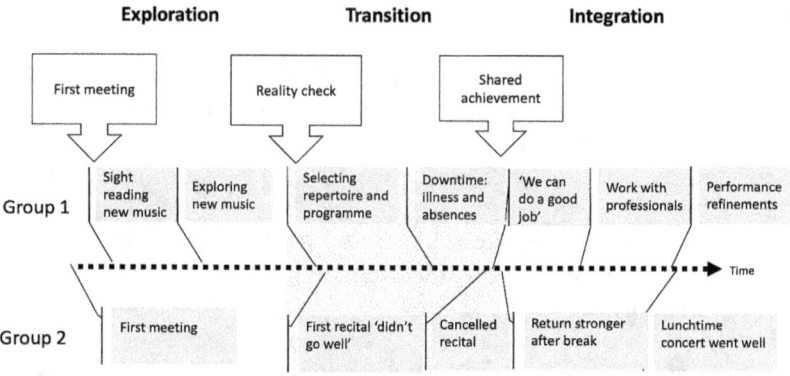

Figure 7.2 Key events in performance preparation as experienced by group members in relation to three phases of development: exploration, transition (grey shaded area), and integration

Source: Pennill, 2019

Vignette 2: the first rehearsal

Taking a perspective in which rehearsal is seen as dynamic and evolving highlights the potential of the first rehearsal of a new group, in which interactions begin to form from the start. In this research, patterns of verbal behaviour appeared within 1 minute (Group 2), and 2 minutes (Group 1).

In Group 1, the patterned exchanges were as follows:

ALL	Laughter and excited chatter
Soprano	Makes a practical suggestion
Alto	Makes counter suggestion
Tenor	Makes a joke or funny remark

This exchange occurred three times during the first rehearsal, at 2 minutes, 15 minutes, and 27 minutes. It illustrates how, without conscious awareness, patterns form quickly and can set the tone for later sessions. In this first session, the immediate focus was on trying out new repertoire and to sing together, never having met before: as a group member described 'sort of note-bashing while we got to know each other' (Soprano, Group 1), using tried and tested methods they had each experienced before in other settings. In both groups there was a mix of this focused task-driven activity and light-hearted social chatter. There was also an acknowledgement that tacit judgements were being made, and that this was a period of delicate balance for the group: 'the social skills to get to know each other, and be sensitive of each other' (Tenor, Group 2). As a result, group members tended to make tentative suggestions, rather than express strong views. A comparison of strategies over the series of rehearsals showed that in the first rehearsal there was more focus on basic technical issues such as getting entries together, resolving major pitching issues, and balancing voices. Later rehearsals featured more comments related to expressive and interpretative elements.

Discussion of main findings

The results of this research suggest that communication and development in these newly formed groups was dynamic and non-linear, progressing through distinct stages alongside more gradual, incremental change. This fits with theories of team development, including Tuckman's well-established model (Tuckman, 1965; Tuckman & Jensen, 1977), which proposes four phases of 'forming', 'storming', 'norming', and performing' (and sometimes a fifth, 'adjourning') to describe how groups go through progressive stages where their personal interactions change in character – for example 'storming' is associated with conflict and discord. Whilst this has some resonance for the phases observed in my research, a more dynamic perspective is reflected in the 'punctuated equilibrium' model (Gersick, 1988, 1989), in which, rather than a linear progression, a steady state exists, from which sudden, rapid change is triggered by accumulated small pressures, for example the time pressure of an approaching deadline. In this model, the change is described as 'revolutionary', and major transitions are frequently observed around the midpoint of any fixed time period. This phenomenon, known as 'temporal pacing' (Gersick, 1994) can lead to major change and moments of major progress in groups. The three phases identified in this study, with its transitions and events, and a marked shift halfway through the preparation period, can perhaps then be best explained by reference to this second model.

Conclusion and implications for practice

The dynamics of rehearsal are complex and evolving, as groups move through change together over time. Considering where rehearsals are on an evolving timeline creates new perspectives for reflection, learning, and teaching. In the early stages there may be uncertainty and unpredictability, resulting from the intermingling of previous experiences. Once established, sudden changes may occur, associated with *transition points* observed in the groups, where they experienced rapid progression from one phase to the next. Later stages are more predictable, as the group is more established in its ways of working. More aligned behaviour provides momentum and stability, with a greater resistance to change and the effects of external forces, in readiness for the performance ahead.

What does this mean in practice? As well as the wider implications of considering ensemble-as-team and building on knowledge of groups of people who collaborate, there are some key implications for ensemble members and teachers to help maximise the chances of successful rehearsals: First rehearsals can set the tone, so efforts made to establish ways of working and make social as well as musical contact will pay dividends later. Fostering discussion, especially early on, can be very constructive, with the knowledge that later rehearsals will have longer episodes of music making, with less verbal exchange.

Where there are time constraints, ensemble members may anticipate shifting group dynamics over time, as described in the three phases, and where changes can happen rapidly. Being prepared for potential differences of opinion and accepting and dealing with them as part of development can therefore be helpful in the knowledge that active discussion and different views contribute to creativity and artistic choices.

For teachers and coaches, considering each stage of rehearsal in relation to the three phases can help to provide a guide to what to expect, and the timing and type of support that may be most effective. In particular, groups may be most able and willing to assimilate external input during the middle 'transition' phase, which is the time of least certainty. By contrast, it may be most helpful to offer gentle guidance at the start, giving time and space in the early stages for interaction patterns to form, especially in new groups, and in the latter stages when nonverbal aspects of performance are becoming embedded.

The ways that ensembles evolve and develop is of interest not only to musicians but also to those involved in group research in other disciplines. Future study can extend the timeline and the types and sizes of groups considered to explore how widely the three phases apply. There is also potential to investigate further the individual contributions and roles of ensemble members – for example, considering the contribution of personality traits as they apply to ensemble interactions. The special case of the first rehearsal is of particular interest, as musicians so often find themselves working on new projects, with new people. Considering the factors which contribute to later success would have potential value for musicians and educators to prepare well and plan effective rehearsals.

Being part of ensembles is integral to many musicians' lives, and there are opportunities to strengthen awareness and teaching of skills relating to group participation (Ginsborg & Wistreich, 2010). Musicians and teachers can support this aim by fostering discussion and building awareness and knowledge of how group processes can help to foster successful ensemble music making.

Main points

- Performance preparation unfolds over time, shaped by key events, group interactions, and external constraints.
- The balance of communication tends to shift from verbal to nonverbal interactions as performance approaches.
- Parallels between effective ensemble rehearsal and team organisation reinforce the mutually transferable nature of the skills and processes involved.

References

Bischof, N., Comi, A., & Eppler, M. J. (2011). Knowledge visualization in qualitative methods – or how can I see what I say? In *2011 15th international conference on information visualisation* (pp. 371–376). IEEE. https://ieeexplore.ieee.org/document/6004069

D'Amario, S., Howard, D. M., Daffern, H., & Pennill, N. (2018). A longitudinal study of intonation in an *a cappella* singing quintet. *Journal of Voice, 34*(1), 159.e13–159.e27. https://doi.org/10.1016/j.jvoice.2018.07.015

Davidson, J., & Good, J. M. M. (2002). Social and musical co-ordination between members of a string quartet: An exploratory study. *Psychology of Music, 30*(2), 186–201. https://doi.org/10.1177/0305735602302005

Ericsson, K. A., Hoffman, R. R., Kozbelt, A., & Williams, A.M. (Eds.). (2018). *The Cambridge handbook of expertise and expert performance.* Cambridge University Press.

Farley, S., Evison, R., Rackham, N., Nicolson, R., & Dawson, J. (2018). The behaviour analysis coding system. In E. Brauner, M. Boos, & M. Kolbe (Eds.), *The Cambridge handbook of group interaction analysis* (pp. 584–593). Cambridge University Press.

Fiore, S. M., & Salas, E. (2006). Team cognition and expert teams: Developing insights from cross – disciplinary analysis of exceptional teams. *International Journal of Sport and Exercise Psychology, 4*(4), 369–375. https://doi.org/10.1080/1612197X.2006.9671803

Gersick, C. J. G. (1988). Time and transition in work teams: Toward a new model of group development. *Academy of Management Journal, 31*(1), 9–41. https://doi.org/10.5465/256496

Gersick, C. J. G. (1989). Marking time: Predictable transitions in task groups. *Academy of Management Journal, 32*(2), 274–309. https://doi.org/10.5465/256363

Gersick, C. J. G. (1994). Pacing strategic change: The case of a new venture. *Academy of Management Journal, 37*(1), 9–45. https://doi.org/10.5465/256768

Gilboa, A., & Tal-Shmotkin, M. (2012). String quartets as self-managed teams: An interdisciplinary perspective. *Psychology of Music, 40*(1), 19–41. https://doi.org/10.1177/0305735610377593

Ginsborg, J., & Wistreich, R. (2010). Promoting excellence in small group music performance: Teaching, learning and assessment. *Royal Northern College of Music accessed, 3,* 2014.

King, E., & Gritten, A. (2017). Communication and interaction in ensemble performance. In J. Rink (Ed.), *Musicians in the making: Pathways to creative performance* (pp. 306–321). Oxford University Press.

Kokotsaki, D. (2007). Understanding the ensemble pianist: A theoretical framework. *Psychology of Music, 35*(4), 641–668. https://doi.org/10.1177/0305735607077835

Magnusson, M. S. (2000). Discovering hidden time patterns in behavior: T-patterns and their detection. *Behavior Research Methods, Instruments, & Computers, 32*(1), 93–110. https://doi.org/10.3758/BF03200792

Mckinney, E. H., Jr., Barker, J. R., Davis, K. J., & Smith, D. (2005). How swift starting action teams get off the ground: What united flight 232 and airline flight crews can tell us about team communication. *Management Communication Quarterly, 19*(2), 198–237. https://doi.org/10.1177/0893318905278539

Pennill, N. (2019). *Ensembles working towards performance: Emerging coordination and interactions in self-organised groups* [Doctoral thesis, The University of Sheffield]. https://etheses.whiterose.ac.uk/25132/1/NicolaPennill_PhDthesis_October2019.pdf

Schütz, A. (1951). Making music together: A study in social relationship. *Social Research, 18,* 76–97. www.jstor.org/stable/40969255

Seddon, F., & Biasutti, M. (2009). A comparison of modes of communication between members of a string quartet and a jazz sextet. *Psychology of Music, 37*(4), 395–415. https://doi.org/10.1177/0305735608100375

Tuckman, B. (1965). Developmental sequence in small groups. *Psychological Bulletin, 63*(6), 384–399. https://doi.org/10.1037/h0022100

Tuckman, B., & Jensen, M. A. C. (1977). Stages of small-group development revisited. *Group Organization Studies, 2*(4), 419–427. https://doi.org/10.1177/105960117700200404

8 Conductors as teachers

The effects of verbal feedback on singers' confidence, enjoyment, and performance quality

Michael Bonshor

Introduction

As a conductor of leisure music groups, I have often been approached by amateur singers to discuss their experiences of either losing or gaining confidence, and to seek advice about this. My previous research (Bonshor, 2002) indicated that many amateur singers experience confidence issues which are serious enough to limit their participation in singing groups or reduce their enjoyment of performing. This is a pity as, for many people, the most accessible way of making music together is through singing in choirs (Pitts, 2005).

As a young musician, I was a multi-instrumentalist, but it was through my experience of group singing that I learnt the most about sight reading, memorising music, expressive performance, and collaborative music making. Having initially been a reluctant singer, I quickly appreciated the value of participating in choirs, and the skills I learnt through this were vital in my performing and teaching career. However, when I first started conducting, it took me a while to realise that leading an amateur ensemble of singers has much in common with teaching a group singing lesson, especially if most of the performers have previously received limited musical or vocal training. One of the key components of effective teaching is providing constructive feedback, which contains specific information about achievements and areas requiring improvement, and which suggests ways of making progress (Hattie & Timperley, 2007). The research data presented later in this chapter indicate that, by using this core teaching skill effectively, conductors can make a significant contribution to learning and confidence building in adult amateur choirs.

Previously published literature on conducting mirrors my own delayed recognition of the teaching and feedback roles played by

DOI: 10.4324/9781003108382-11

effective conductors. There are some studies which frame conducting as teaching in formal educational settings (Yarbrough & Madsen, 1998), but conducting in the wider context of adult amateur and professional ensembles is usually discussed in terms of musical leadership (Jansson, 2013) and general leadership philosophies (Bass & Riggio, 2006) rather than pedagogy or teaching style. Books on conducting also tend to foreground the conductor's leadership rather than their teaching style. This may be because writers on this topic often focus on those who conduct professional ensembles, in which there is rarely any expectation of explicit teaching, and there is little literature on conducting amateur singers.

My professional practice and observations of fellow practitioners have raised, for me, many questions about the psychology and philosophy of teaching amateur singers, whether during individual lessons, or when teaching through conducting ensembles. One of the questions that has kept arising in my work has been 'How can conductors help singers to increase their confidence while rehearsing and performing?' In this chapter, I will report the findings of a project designed to find some answers to this question.

Summary of the research

The research aims were to identify the main factors affecting confidence amongst adult amateur singers in a wide range of group singing activities, and to use the research findings to extrapolate some practical recommendations for conductors working with amateur singing groups.

Method

Because of the personal nature of the voice as an individual, embodied instrument (Thurman & Welch, 2000), and the subjective nature of self-reported confidence levels, I decided that a qualitative methodology would be most appropriate. Interviews and focus groups would give singers an opportunity to voice some of their concerns, and to share some of their own strategies for managing confidence issues.

I recorded three focus group interviews with a total of 18 participants, followed by a further 16 interviews with individual singers. I used a semi-structured format, which allowed space for the participants to introduce topics that I had not necessarily anticipated. Over 40 hours of verbal data were obtained, which I transcribed and analysed using Interpretative Phenomenological Analysis (Smith et al.,

2009). Some quotations from the interviews are included in this chapter, and all participants have been given pseudonyms to preserve their anonymity.

All 34 participants had extensive experience of group singing; all except one had been members of choirs for at least ten years, and 23 of the participants each had over 15 years of relevant experience. They had all sung with several different conductors and between them they represented a variety of amateur choirs (including community choirs, choral societies, operatic societies, and musical theatre companies) throughout the UK. All participants displayed a strong commitment to their leisure singing activities, but only two interviewees had received any formal musical education beyond secondary school. Most participants had received no individual musical or vocal training during their school years and reported having received very limited musical education in the classroom.

The findings included several different factors affecting singers' confidence (Bonshor, 2014), including group dynamics within the choir, the effects of choral acoustics and choir layout, and the body language of conductors and fellow singers. This chapter, however, focuses specifically on the effect of verbal feedback provided by the conductor. In the following section I will present some of the participants' views of how the conductor's feedback and communication style can affect confidence levels in amateur vocal ensembles. I will then discuss the implications of these findings and suggest some practical applications.

Findings

When I asked the participants to tell me about people who had influenced their confidence, either positively or negatively, the majority mentioned conductors. When examining conductors' communication with singers, many researchers have tended to focus on the influence of conducting gestures on choral performance quality (Fuelberth, 2003; Grady, 2014). However, the interviewees in my research project barely mentioned conducting gestures. Instead, they focused on the conductors' verbal communication, and the effect that it has upon their learning and confidence. Verbal feedback plays an important psychological and pedagogical role in formal education (Hattie & Timperley, 2007), and my participants reported that verbal feedback from conductors has a similarly powerful impact.

Many of the participants recognised that conductor communication can create either a virtuous or a vicious cycle in which verbal feedback, learning, performance quality, and confidence become interdependent. They also felt that the authority traditionally invested in conductors means that their feedback has a particularly strong effect on singers' confidence. Because conductors, like teachers, are usually seen as experts in their field, their criticism or praise is taken to heart and can have long-lasting emotional and motivational effects:

> The conductor at the time said, 'You're one of my best sopranos,' which was a real boost, you know. And I thought 'Wow! That's wonderful!' And then I thought 'Well, I must keep this up'.
>
> (Pamela)

Music students in formal education have previously reported that they would prefer it if their conductors (who are also often their teachers) spent less time talking and more time allowing the groups to make music (Nápoles & Vázquez-Ramos, 2013). However, the adult amateur participants in my study expressed a desire for more verbal communication from their conductors, to enhance their learning. They wanted their conductors to provide greater quantities of both praise and constructive criticism, plus more specific details in both positive and negative feedback to enable the singers either to maintain or improve their performance:

> You don't get the constructive criticism [. . .] And you know [fellow singer] and I are always chatting, and [he'll] say 'That was crap!' And I'll say, 'It was crap!' ((laughs)) And [conductor] will say 'That's all right. That's nice'.
>
> (Frank)

Although my participants wanted more verbal feedback from their conductors, they felt that indiscriminate, routine praise was likely to be insincere, and caused them to question the conductor's judgement. This sometimes led to a sense of mistrust around the conductor's credibility, so that genuine compliments were not taken seriously, and they started to doubt themselves:

> [Conductor] could be very fulsome in her praise after a concert. . . . It was always the best concert ever, so . . . you never knew . . . if there was any truth in it.
>
> (Barbara)

It was also felt that some criticism can be profoundly destructive, with many singers reporting situations in which this had adversely affected their learning and confidence. Singling out individuals or small groups of singers was universally seen as unproductive and demotivating. In extreme cases, some people had left choirs (or seen other singers leave) after receiving particularly harsh personalised criticism from the conductor:

> She [conductor] would pick people out and criticise and the pressure got so great I thought I'd burst. She had a go at one of my friends and she [my friend] said, 'I don't like this'. And I said, 'No, I don't like this'. So, we both made a joint decision that we wouldn't go anymore, and it was such a relief.
>
> (Nora)

Whether criticism is interpreted as constructive or destructive partly depends upon how the feedback is delivered. The importance of mutual respect was a common theme, with a disconcerting proportion of singers reporting a lack of respect from their conductors when delivering feedback. The most extreme cases included 'sarcasm', 'shouting and stomping', 'personal attacks', 'having paddies' and 'hissy fits' when a measured approach would be more appropriate.

Some participants attributed unconstructive communication styles to their conductors' lack of recognition of the needs of adult singers, who are making music voluntarily as part of their leisure; they expect to enjoy the activity, and to be treated as responsible adults, as well as learning new skills. One participant compared an attitude that can be interpreted as patronising, with a more respectful approach which allows any negative feedback to be focused on the task rather than the person:

> [Conductors] sometimes ((assumes schoolmasterly tone)) 'Now we're going to have to bash through this to get this one right!' ((Groans)). So, it needs to be the positive, musical approach. And not the blamey approach. It's the approach that says, 'I'm all right and you're all right'. Not 'I'm all right but you lot are not. I've got to work on you!'
>
> (Harry)

The interpretation of, and response to, verbal feedback from the conductor is affected by individual differences (Bonshor, 2017), including the singer's baseline self-confidence, (Hattie & Timperley,

2007) as well as their age, personality, and life experience. Reasons for participating in group singing also vary; for example, some adult amateur singers are keen to learn about musical terminology or vocal technique, whilst others prefer to concentrate on singing new repertoire, revisiting favourite songs, or socialising with their peers. In addition, the membership of each singing group is inherently diverse, and adult learners' individual needs and priorities vary significantly (Findsen, 2005). This means that, among the conductor's many skills, it is important to develop a finely honed ability to perceive and understand the needs of the singers, to develop a flexible approach to teaching through conducting, and to tailor the verbal feedback to the needs of the singers.

Although conductors play a key role in providing effective and supportive teaching in amateur adult choirs, they are not the only source of verbal communication and learning. All participants also mentioned four main aspects of group interaction in choirs, which can beneficially or adversely affect their learning, performance quality, and confidence: role modelling by other singers; reciprocal support and verbal encouragement; informal mentoring; and peer feedback.

An important message here is that, although the amount, content, and style of delivery of the conductor's feedback is crucial, it is not the only influence upon the learning, confidence, and performance of the choir. The conductor might be providing exemplary feedback but, if the interactions between singers are not supportive, or individuals do not react positively to constructive feedback, the choir will not thrive without fundamental changes in the group dynamics (Bonshor, 2014).

Vignettes

Vignette 1: Angela

When asked about influences upon their confidence, some participants directly mentioned a desire for their conductors to provide a greater quantity of constructive criticism and meaningful praise in rehearsals: For example, Angela, who sings with a large choral society conducted by schoolteachers, felt that the singers would benefit from more praise in order to support their learning:

> I think sometimes, with adults, people's transition into 'I'm OK with children but now I'm dealing with adults' is tricky, and they forget that we want to be praised as well.

She also found it difficult to trust conductors who gave small amounts of vague feedback, and interpreted this negatively:

> Choral society feedback? They'll just say, 'There were some good things in it'. This is what we get from [our conductor] – 'There were some very good things in there'. So, you know it wasn't very good.

Angela valued constructive criticism, but felt that it should be balanced with positive feedback, as leisure choirs prioritise enjoyment as well as (and in some cases more than) performance quality:

> I do like it when [conductors] say something positive. It may be rubbish, but there must be something positive about it. [. . .] Given that it's a pleasure, it's a hobby, it's in your free time [. . .]. And, yes, criticise. Yes, be constructive with your criticism. That's absolutely fine. But please find something nice to say. We want to come out of it on a high.

Her recommendations for teaching through providing effective feedback are expressed in a light-hearted way. However, she is making strong points about achieving a healthy balance of praise and criticism, delivered in an appropriate style:

> I think one word of encouragement, and two words of explanation that we can understand, and six criticisms is a formula! I think just one bit of praise will cover quite a lot of other stuff, but don't just keep ((impersonates conductor growling and cracking the whip)). And, not be patronising, but be clear with your explanation [. . .]. Praise of any sort is what everybody thrives on, you know – even the dog!

Angela appreciated the style of a new conductor who included more explicit teaching in the rehearsals:

> Instead of just [using musical terms] and expecting that we all know, he's actually explaining it. And he's doing it as a teacher more. [. . .] And it's much better if somebody does that with you and doesn't assume that everybody in the masses knows what it's all about.

Vignette 2: Tim

Although Tim is a singer with a long history of performing with amateur musical theatre societies, he has received minimal musical training and largely relies upon the conductor to teach him the repertoire. If he feels that insufficient time has been spent on this in rehearsals, he finds it difficult to perform confidently:

> My confidence depended on how well I knew the music. If I knew I knew the music, my confidence was fine. If I knew I was going to struggle with some bits of the music, my confidence would decrease.

Tim emphasised the importance of the conductor's attitude toward the singers, and felt that singling people out for criticism was always counterproductive:

> I think if the Musical Director is welcoming and encouraging, and not scathing or picking out individuals, that makes a huge difference. You feel confident then. If it's a [musical director] that picks out individuals – even if it's just to say 'Right. The tenors do this line'. And then one person at a time does that line, I feel that's picking on people. I'm not comfortable with that.

He felt disoriented and unsupported when there was a lack of feedback about the group's progress:

> Thinking about a show recently that I did, the [musical director] was very quiet and didn't say much, and that felt . . . That didn't feel right.

However, he was also clear that continual, non-specific praise was meaningless and undermined the conductor's credibility:

> If you're working with somebody that continually says 'That's good. That's good. That's good', you find yourself thinking 'Is it?'

For Tim to take feedback seriously and learn from it, he needed to trust the judgement of feedback providers, based on their own reputation for expertise, experience, and/or skill:

> Appraisal from the people who I know know what they're talking about, be it a teacher or a fellow singer, but as long as I know they know what they're talking about.

This was a common theme and reinforces the old but true adage about the relationship between great power and great responsibility. Conductors, teachers, and other experienced musicians may sometimes forget that they are seen as experts and role models, and that their words consequently carry a great deal of weight in terms of affecting learning, performance, and confidence.

Conclusion and implications

The findings from this research support some of the intuitions that I had during my conducting career and build on Price and Byo's (2002) suggestion that 'everything involved in rehearsing and conducting can be characterised by a teaching paradigm' (p. 336). They note that, in school music settings, rehearsing and teaching are often seen as analogous, but that this is not always the case in adult music making. My findings have identified that adult amateur singers derive confidence from conductors who teach effectively, and that providing constructive feedback is a key component of successful teaching in this context. This research has led to the following recommendations for providing feedback for effective learning, enjoyable rehearsing, and confident performing in adult amateur choirs.

Recognising the powerful influence of conductor feedback and the responsibility that this places upon the conductor is an important step toward providing feedback in a way which adds value to the experience of rehearsing and performing. The next step is to consider how verbal feedback contributes to morale and learning. The content of feedback is clearly important in all teaching situations, including rehearsals. However, other key components include providing a well-balanced amount of constructive criticism and praise; providing specific, task-orientated feedback rather than general or person-oriented feedback; and delivering the feedback in a style that is respectful and meaningful.

Feedback also needs to be pitched at an appropriate level for the particular group being conducted, as amateur groups vary widely and may include singers with a range of different skills, experiences, and musical knowledge. The feature that most share, however, is a need for music making to be an enjoyable, shared experience, and the way in which verbal feedback is phrased and delivered can contribute to this.

When working under time pressure and carrying out all the necessary multi-tasking, conductors may sometimes find it difficult to remember to do all of this. However, rehearsal planning could include marking the score with teaching points, indicating when feedback could be provided during the session, and some thoughts about how to phrase and deliver meaningful feedback. In my own teaching and conducting practice, I have found it useful to take a few moments to consider which specific aspects I am praising or criticising. Once I have asked myself 'What exactly was so good about that performance?' I find that I can give more precisely tailored praise that will help the singers to repeat their success. Similarly, if I ask myself 'Why was that rendition less successful?' I can provide constructive criticism designed to help the group to focus on how to improve their performance rather than dwelling on the negative feelings evoked by poor performance. These evaluative questions may also lead me to identify areas in which I need to either maintain or adapt my communication content and style.

Although the conductor usually bears the main responsibility for facilitating confident learning and performance, interactions between choir members also have an effect (Bonshor, 2016). Group dynamics can be negative as well as positive and are not always within the control of the conductor. However, monitoring group interactions may mean that problems are identified and addressed before they escalate, inhibit learning, and reduce morale. The conductor often has a limited influence on these peer interactions and, especially where there are committees or other mechanisms for support, negative group dynamics are likely to be tackled most effectively as a team effort.

Individual differences between singers can affect their responses to receiving feedback, and these need to be considered when delivering criticism and praise. Some people appreciate plain speaking and others are more sensitive to perceived criticism. It is helpful to maintain an awareness of this and to be prepared to adapt communication and teaching styles accordingly. Also, some groups may share preconceived ideas and expectations which affect their interpretation of feedback, and teaching points, perhaps based on experiences with previous conductors. For conductors who are new to a group, it can be useful to explain their approach to giving (and perhaps receiving!) feedback so that misunderstandings are less likely to happen.

The findings of this research relate to adult amateur choirs, but many of the points about feedback and facilitation are likely to be relevant to other musical ensembles too, as well as to other teaching situations. Whenever groups are making music together, constructive feedback from a trusted source is a powerful tool which can expedite learning, boost self-confidence, enhance performance quality, and add to the enjoyment of the experience.

Main points

- Framing conducting as teaching in amateur choirs can contribute to a supportive and productive learning environment.
- The quality, content, and delivery of verbal feedback from conductors has a strong impact on learning and confidence in adult amateur singers.
- Because conductors are perceived as 'musical experts', their verbal feedback has a particularly powerful and lasting influence on learning, performance quality, and confidence amongst adult amateur singers.
- The amount, content, and style of delivery of verbal feedback all have an impact on how the feedback is interpreted by the recipients.
- The most effective verbal feedback is genuine, specific, and respectfully delivered.
- Praise is meaningful when it is perceived as realistic, proportionate to achievement, and provides exact details so that the achievement can be repeated.
- Criticism is most effective when it is task-oriented rather than person-oriented and includes constructive suggestions for improvement.
- Developing a rehearsal plan which includes giving constructive feedback and teaching points will support effective learning and confidence building in amateur choirs.

References

Bass, B. M., & Riggio, R. E. (2006). *Transformational leadership*. Psychology Press.

Bonshor, M. J. (2002). *Musical performance anxiety amongst adult amateur singers: The effects of age, experience and training* [Unpublished master's dissertation, The University of Sheffield].

Bonshor, M. J. (2014). *Confidence and the choral singer: The effects of choir configuration, collaboration and communication* [Doctoral dissertation, University of Sheffield]. http://etheses.whiterose.ac.uk/7230/

Bonshor, M. (2016). Sharing knowledge and power in adult amateur choral communities: The impact of communal learning on the experience of musical participation. *International Journal of Community Music, 9*(3), 291–305. https://doi.org/10.1386/ijcm.9.3.291_1

Bonshor, M. (2017). *The confident choir: A handbook for leaders of group singing*. Rowman and Littlefield.

Findsen, B. (2005). *Learning later*. Krieger Publishing Company.

Fuelberth, R. J. V. (2003). The effect of conducting gesture on singers' perceptions of inappropriate vocal tension. *International Journal of Research in Choral Singing, 1*(1), 13–21.

Grady, M. L. (2014). Effects of traditional pattern, lateral-only, and vertical-only conducting gestures on acoustic and perceptual measures of choir sound: An exploratory study. *International Journal of Research in Choral Singing, 5*(1), 39–59.

Hattie, J., & Timperley, H. (2007). The power of feedback. *Review of Educational Research, 77*(1), 81–112. https://doi.org/10.3102/003465430298487

Jansson, D. (2013). *Musical leadership: The choral conductor as sensemaker and liberator* [Doctoral dissertation, Norges musikkhøgskole]. https://nmh.brage.unit.no/nmh-xmlui/handle/11250/172455

Nápoles, J., & Vázquez-Ramos, A. M. (2013). Perceptions of time spent in teacher talk: A comparison among self-estimates, peer estimates, and actual time. *Journal of Research in Music Education, 60*(4), 452–461. https://doi.org/10.1177/0022429412463246

Pitts, S. E. (2005). *Valuing musical participation.* Ashgate Publishing Ltd.

Price, H. E., & Byo, J. L. (2002). Rehearsing and conducting. In R. Parncutt & G. E. McPherson (Eds.), *The science and psychology of music performance* (pp. 269–283). Oxford University Press.

Smith, J. A., Flowers, P., & Larkin, M. (2009). *Interpretative phenomenological analysis.* SAGE.

Thurman, L., & Welch, G. F. (2000). *Bodymind and voice: Foundations of voice education* (2nd ed.). National Center for Voice and Speech.

Yarbrough, C., & Madsen, K. (1998). The evaluation of teaching in choral rehearsals. *Journal of Research in Music Education, 46*(4), 469–481. https://doi.org/10.2307/3345344

Part IV
Strategies for enhancing musical confidence and enjoyment

9 Singing and signing with Deaf and hearing impaired young people

Gail Dudson

Introduction

The study of music and Deaf[1] people has a small but long history. Deafness has historically been viewed as a deficit model where music was regarded as therapy, in contrast to the contemporary social model of Deafness as a linguistic minority and culture. There has been little research into Deaf and Hearing Impaired (DHI) people's music making, with some notable exceptions. A remarkable study from 1848 documented a deaf woman learning music to a high degree of proficiency through successful teaching strategies (Turner, 1848). In 1939 Wecker demonstrated that deaf children could recognise and replicate pulse, rhythm, and pitch, through careful choice of medium and method (Wecker, 1939). In 'The Challenge of the Exceptional Child' (Cruickshank, 1952) we see advocacy for what is now called inclusive practice: that acceptance, adjustment, and changed attitudes lead to equality, and that DHI children should participate in music for its own sake, rather than for therapy.

But mainstream change takes time. Alice-Ann Darrow (1985, 1987, 1999) explored ideas of music and its place within Deaf culture, finding among DHI people a preference for playing rather than listening, and objections to music being presented as primarily therapeutic. She also documented differences between DHI people's ideas about music for themselves, when compared to hearing people's ideas about what music should be like for DHI people.

Still though, there was little representation from people who were Deaf, though Deaf professional musicians were emerging. In her TED talk, professional percussionist Evelyn Glennie (2003) explained how she had explored and developed her sensitivity and responses to vibration, as her hearing system. There are now Deaf professional musicians who are often involved in teaching, and are articulating

DOI: 10.4324/9781003108382-13

the Deaf experience of music performance, appreciation, and musical learning.

> Deafness is poorly understood in general. For instance, there is a common misconception that deaf people live in a world of silence. To understand the nature of deafness, first one has to understand the nature of hearing.
>
> (Glennie, 2003)

Summary of the research

This research was part of a project to explore the personal, social, and musical engagement of Deaf young people in Singing and Signing, an important part of Deaf culture and education. As singing is often among young people's earliest musical experience, it is vital in developing musical skills, understanding, and the ability to live a full musical life.

The study set out to explore effective strategies for teaching Deaf young people music skills of pitch, pulse, rhythm, and expression and to investigate how British Sign Language (BSL) can be made 'musical'. The study followed the progress of weekly Singing and Signing sessions over two terms in a School for the Deaf, with participants ranging from 5–19-year-olds, and where BSL was the primary language of the school community. BSL is the language of Deaf people in the UK; a visual and gestural language, it needs no speech, and has grammar, syntax and structure which are different from spoken English.

The study did not take account of the specific hearing capacities of the participants, though almost all previous studies into Deaf people and music have done so. This was deliberate; hearing children are not tested when they choose to join in music making, and they are free to make their own listening, playing, and participation choices. My research presupposed that Deaf children should be similarly treated; what the child feels, hears, and responds to is what is important, more than a clinical test. Individuals' hearing capability measures (audiograms) were not used to form any baseline assessment or suitability for participation, though individual needs were taken into account in music sessions. Some participants had assistive devices – hearing aids or cochlear implants – whilst others had none.

The project was led by a Deaf professional musician, Paul Whittaker OBE, a leading interpreter of signed song who supported and trained hearing singing leaders who delivered weekly sessions. The school staff, both Deaf and hearing, joined in every session, supporting both singing leaders and children in their learning. The sessions were dynamic and iterative, as music leaders changed and adapted their teaching practice to find what worked best.

The study sought insights into music making from Deaf young people, Deaf singing leaders, and Deaf professional musicians. The research was exploratory, focusing on the experience of participation, how engagement was enabled, and what activities were effective, rather than measures of progress through testing.

Exploring teaching strategies

For hearing children, music (and indeed speech) is something they hear before they try to do it, by copying. For Deaf children, such information gathering is mostly visual, and the 'copying' mode of learning is less open to them. Hearing children who learn music through a structured pedagogical process are taught about a sense of pulse early, as is the case in both the Kodály approach and Dalcroze Eurhythmics. These pedagogies use visual signals and somatic practice to embody musical principles and instil musicianship, and this also worked well for Deaf young people in the sessions I observed: clapping, moving, walking, and 'action' songs where pulse, rhythm, and pitch could be visually or gesturally expressed were effective (e.g., Bounce High, Bounce Low, a three-pitch song in which a ball is bounced to emphasise pulse). Through the regular use of a small set of activities, participants began to say they could 'detect' pulse and understand it and learned to choose and correctly indicate a pulse tempo when it was their turn to lead an activity.

To introduce rhythm, notation was used from the outset, as it provided a visual explanation of the principles. Participants could see the rhythmic patterns and then create their own, so learning the building blocks of bars, 4-bar phrases, and 16-bar forms through notation. Even the youngest participants became excellent at this, using symbols in a variety of ways, building phrases and using rhythm imaginatively, including starting a pattern with a rest. They were able to notate a pattern from watching it being clapped. Participants were also very quick to learn to recognise a song from notated rhythm symbols: five out of ten children had raised their hands within ten seconds to recognise the rhythm pattern for 'Pease Pudding Hot' in a class toward the end of the project. These successes led the music leaders to go further and try some basic song-writing with the children. Participants first wrote a rhythm and then added words; the results showed a good grasp of syllable stress and the ability to put words into an appropriate rhythm pattern.

It was not unexpected that in singing, vocalising, and pitching sounds participants made progress at different rates. It was evident early in the study that participants had very different styles and confidence with vocalisation or singing, and that, generally, younger children were less familiar and comfortable with vocalising. The aim was finding a natural voice, volume control, and some pitch differentiation, rather than vocal training. School staff said that participants vocalised more in singing and signing than in any other activity.

Teaching pitch to Deaf young people also presented many challenges, as although the idea of pitch can be shown visually (by up and down movements), it is not as directly translatable from the visual, when compared to pulse and rhythm, where even rhythmic mood can be conveyed relatively easily – by 'marching', for example. There was success initially in finding pitch differences in voices through musical games. 'Rockets' – tracing a trajectory of a firework with a finger and following the pitch with the voice – resulted in pitch-shifting vocalisation by eight out of nine primary aged participants and increased the volume of vocalisation from participants' usual level. Teaching songs was the main vehicle for developing a sense of pitch. Almost all participants grasped and copied pitch variations using two or three pitches, and by the end of the project had developed the ability to control pitch in their own voice and use different pitches.

A small number of the participants showed particular musical aptitude, grasping the principles of pulse, rhythm, and pitch quickly, and making quick progress, observed by music leaders and the author. Deafness seemed not to inhibit musical facility in the ways that are often assumed by hearing people. One 11-year-old boy, for example, could sing a song well, at exactly the pitch used by music leaders, and at tempo, even when he had not heard it for some weeks.

Making BSL musical

In addition to the short songs for teaching musical concepts, the participants also learned some standard repertoire children's songs. Songs with a strong rhythmic element, with stories or events that could easily be visualised, and were useful for everyday life, worked well.

Music leaders worked both with and without backing tracks when teaching and practising songs. There was no discernible difference in the ability of the participants to complete a song with or without, though working without a backing track gave the hearing music leaders the opportunity to change the tempo and the pitch of a song to suit participants. All song practice was conducted in ways which facilitated participation; a leader would stand within the vision of all participants, give countdown signals for entry at the beginning and between verses, and would then sign and sing the song along with the participants.

Songs with relevant or interesting themes for the age group worked well. 'A B-U-G' was a favourite and included a rare opportunity for finger spelling. One singing leader observed that this song got 100% participation every time. The backing track for this song had a half-speed ending, which the children had learned to replicate perfectly to match the track once the leader had worked out visual signals to facilitate it. Because it had a high degree of repetition, the leader taught the song by getting children to remember just the words which changed in each verse – live, hide, and play, which also prompted the children to sign the other deviating words – carpet, stairs, dark corners.

Both hearing music leaders, Anna Myatt and Natalie Davies, were singers; however, they were used to singing from scores. Signing in BSL needs both hands, which meant working from memory. There was some evidence that even the youngest children had better memory skills than the hearing leaders, perhaps an indication that Deaf people need to develop memory which outstrips their hearing peers; these moments gave the participants the opportunity to shine, and to guide the teacher. This provided two valuable insights: when selecting repertoire, find songs with some degree of repetition but not so much that losing one's place and going round in circles becomes a danger, and that repetitive practice is needed to commit words, melody, rhythm, and signs to memory. This meant that the participants had, by the end of the study, a smaller repertoire of songs learned than would be expected from a group of hearing children.

A further complexity is that BSL's grammar and syntax means that signing is not necessarily in the same order as English wording. Through the project, the characteristics a song would need in order to be suitable became clear, in addition to the usual criteria of suitability for the vocal range, appropriate subject, and right level of musical difficulty for the skills of the participants. Songs worked best when they had a strong narrative or storyline, so that participants could visualise it, and some standard patterns and repetition of words, melody, and rhythm, as singing and signing is done from memory. The words also needed to be suitable for signing – and it takes time to develop the judgement for this, including knowing some BSL syntax and choosing songs where English and BSL word order can be aligned in some way.

In signing, precision matters: handshapes, gesture size, distances, and movement are all fundamental elements; making a cup and a table in the right proportions, showing the size of a caterpillar, the strength of a breeze. Creative signing practice follows the pace and expression of a song and uses signs in a measured way (for example, three signs for each line of song verse) going beyond everyday BSL and making signing rhythmic (or poetic), reinforcing musicality and using gesture and speed of signing to show expression. For very young participants who were learning to sign, breaking standard signing conventions was difficult to understand, even confusing. However, staff liked the creative and poetic elements of signing for songs as it meant the children were learning about the uses of BSL in more than an everyday way.

Engagement and participation

Participation, engagement, enjoyment, and confidence in music were used as the main indicators of social and personal benefit. At the start of the project, rates of participation were high, and attendance was good across age ranges. Engagement was generally energetic and positive, although there was some evidence that older participants were more likely to pick and choose to engage during sessions. Boys' participation was less full, unless they specifically liked the material or the session was led by a male Deaf musician. Younger participants were consistently engaged, hardworking, and generally more enthusiastic about singing, though they said they preferred musical games and rhymes which were more physical, active, and short. It was still the case that boys needed more persuasion and for activities to be fitted to their personal preferences.

The interest and participation of the older participants declined over time, particularly among boys, and when singing sessions were led by female, hearing music leaders. Two boys explained that having learned some useful skills they wanted to move on and learn DJ skills and rap. Having discovered that they could participate in, learn, and perform music, they wanted the musical experiences of a typical teenager.

Half the participants reported that they enjoyed Singing and Signing, with the 14–16-year-old boys most likely to say that it was not for them, signing 'not cool' to each other in a group discussion. During the discussion, however, they were singing and signing unprompted,

Singing and signing with the Deaf 107

remembering well after weeks of non-participation; perhaps their statements were more vehement than their genuine feelings. Similarly, the music leaders reported that whilst Sean (primary aged boy) would say he did not like the project and Kara (primary aged girl) would say she loved it, their behaviour and willingness to participate in sessions differed very little.

Participants showed increased confidence and willingness to lead or co-lead from an early stage, and there were neither age nor sex differences in this aspect (co-leading = one signer, one rhythm leader, one pulse leader). By the end of the study, all the primary children had the skills and confidence to stand in front of their peers and co-lead a song, with or without a backing track.

Vignettes

Case study: Pippa

Pippa was a five-year-old, very active and committed participant. Although she displayed and communicated clear preferences for some activities, she was always engaged, even in songs where BSL signs were stretching her capability and she needed to concentrate hard. As would be expected in a five-year-old, musical games were her favourite and she found 'Bounce High, Bounce Low' most enjoyable. She quickly grasped the concepts of bouncing the ball in time to the pulse, and the cooperation needed for passing the ball to someone else in the circle. Her drawing used correct note values for the game, though the ability to write out note values is not generally demonstrated at this age. Both elements of the rhythm are written out; four crotchets for the first phrase, six quavers and a crotchet for the second, though this second phrase she has written backwards (marked with dots). As she made this drawing (Figure 9.1), I watched her get to the edge of the page, 'turn', and go back to finish the phrase, adding more notes later as decoration.

Pippa had been taken to a Ceilidh by her parents, and they had observed two interesting and new behaviours. First, she showed pleasure at some instruments and displeasure at others, indicating new discernment, and second, she had approached the caller and asked for the microphone so she could sing, performing solo for two minutes in front of an audience. She had vocalised consistently, maintained a constant volume, though her speech articulation was limited. Her performance was well-received by the ceilidh attenders.

Figure 9.1 Pippa's illustration of her favourite song

Vignette: Speech therapy

A speech therapist explained that Deaf young people have varying degrees of speech and vocalisation and offered examples of ways in which the approaches taken to music activities could be copied by therapists as part of speech development. The music leader used coloured mats to mark out pulse, with a different colour for each bar. Syllables of the song lyrics were printed separately and placed on the correct beat by the children. Deaf children can find syllables difficult as neither written English nor mouth movement necessarily illustrate syllables e.g., banana and mum have similar mouth shapes, yet banana has three syllables and mum has one. The therapist considered the approach useful for both learning syllables and for developing speed and pulse in spoken word.

Conclusion and implications for practice

The study was wide-ranging in attempting to consider both the social and musical benefits that Deaf young people can gain from participating in good quality Singing and Signing. It illustrated on a small scale, though very clearly, that Deaf young people enjoy and want to participate in music making. It showed that when music is thoughtfully led and adapted to meet their needs, Deaf young people will work to acquire the skills that enable them to participate in music making.

Successful adaptive practice for teaching Deaf young people included the use of visual and physical strategies to embed musical elements – walking and clapping for pulse, rhythm, and tempo, using coloured mats for each beat. Using conventional notation, particularly note-values, with even the youngest children, allowed them to sing together effectively, and brought confidence through opportunities to lead their peers and invent their own rhythms. Learning was incremental, using games to develop vocalising, and working toward finding a sense of pitch, dynamic and vocal control, before moving on to songs with limited pitches. There were some indications that Deaf children learned pulse and rhythm skills faster than would be expected in their hearing peers, though they took longer to develop a sense of pitch control.

The participants in this study were all Deaf, in a school for the Deaf. In a mixed Deaf and hearing community, some different approaches may be needed. A study comparing Deaf musical learning in different settings may well provide useful information for practitioners about adapting their approaches according to setting and the context for learning.

The study showed some ways in which Deaf young people need adaptations or differences in educational practice to develop their musical learning. The Deaf practitioners knew this already from their personal experience – though there are still too few professional Deaf music practitioners. In order for there to be more Deaf practitioners, music needs to be part of every Deaf child's learning – and for the time being at least there need to be hearing music leaders who can deliver it.

There is still significant research to be done in following the footsteps of Deaf professional musicians, including instrumental learning, vocal training, and the skills of conducting and leading performances. These are all examples of practice where there are Deaf musicians working at a high professional standard, and their journeys have been individual and sometimes made possible by the support of their families and teachers. This small study demonstrates the need for further research to support music educators in designing effective learning activities to bring Deaf young people to a point of musical independence, self-sufficiency, and excellence.

Main points

- Deaf young people show similar variation in musical tastes and preferences to hearing children, developing their own musical aspirations as they learn (such as an interest in DJ skills, rap, and any other musical style).

- Boys seem to prefer active games and short songs to learning longer pieces, in common with their hearing peers.
- Deaf young people may be more confident at leading, co-leading, or performing solos than their hearing peers. Deafness means working together with others can be more difficult than working alone. This is generally the opposite to hearing peers' confidence and behaviour.
- Choosing repertoire very carefully is essential for Singing and Signing; patterns of repetition and fitting signs to pulse or rhythm were important for learning and interest.
- Many standard music learning materials are designed with a specific age group in mind. Learning musical fundamentals when children are older means using different, more age-appropriate materials and repertoire to maintain engagement.

Note

1 Deaf (capitalised) – a minority community with its own culture and language (sign language). Terminology around deafness has changed over time, with Deaf (as a culture) being relatively recent. Current terminology includes deaf, Deaf, and deaf and hearing impaired (DHI). Not all deaf people regard themselves as a member of the Deaf community. Others use the term Deaf and Hearing Impaired (DHI).

References

Cruickshank, W. (1952). The challenge of the exceptional child. *Music Educators Journal*, *38*(6), 18–20. https://doi.org/10.2307/3387625

Darrow, A. (1985). Music for the deaf. *Music Educators Journal*, *71*(6), 33–35. https://doi.org/10.2307/3396472

Darrow, A. (1987). Exploring the arts of sign and song. *Music Educators Journal*, *74*(1), 32–35. https://doi.org/10.2307/3401234

Darrow, A. (1999). Music and deaf culture: Deaf students' perception of emotion in music. *Journal of Music Therapy*, *36*(2), 88–109. https://doi.org/10.1093/jmt/43.1.2

Glennie, E. (2003). *How to truly listen.* www.ted.com/talks/evelyn_glennie_how_to_truly_listen

Turner, W. (1848). Music among the deaf and dumb. *American Annals of the Deaf and Dumb*, *2*(1), 1–6.

Wecker, K. (1939). Music for totally deaf children. *Music Educators Journal*, *25*(6), 45–47. https://doi.org/10.2307/3385404

10 Teaching pre-performance routines to improve students' performance experience

Mary Hawkes

Introduction

The main focus of most writing on piano pedagogy is on learning, practising, and memorising music. What little guidance there is for teachers on preparing pupils for a performance typically consists of advice to 'do your practice' and 'don't be nervous'. Implicit in this is that you learn to perform 'by doing it'. However, this did not work for me. As a teenager I did not enjoy solo piano performance and avoided it as much as possible. These experiences influenced my work when I became a piano teacher. I wanted to find ways to help my students enjoy their performance experience. The breakthrough came when I began to transfer ideas, including pre-performance routines (PPRs), from the tennis court to the piano teachers' studio.

I was working both as a part-time piano teacher and part-time tennis coach in the 1990s. For my professional development in tennis, I undertook a practical sport psychology diploma. It was during these studies that I had a 'lightbulb moment': strategies I was using with my tennis players, to help them cope with performance pressures and achieve their performance potential, were also applicable to my piano pupils. At first, I used the techniques I was learning with one piano student, and gradually I introduced the idea of deliberately teaching performance preparation strategies to all my pupils. Teaching and practising routines became a significant part of that preparation. I instinctively felt that this was beneficial, but it was during my research that I was able to investigate this systematically.

A PPR is a particular type of routine defined in sport as 'a sequence of task relevant thoughts and actions which an athlete engages in systematically prior to his or her performance' (Moran, 1996, p. 177). PPRs are used before self-paced acts, defined as 'actions that are carried out largely at one's own speed and without interference from other people' (Moran, 2004, loc.2965). Performing music as a soloist or in small groups is a self-paced act where the individual or group are in charge of the speed at which they begin to play, as well as the thoughts and actions that they have immediately prior to the performance. This suggests that PPRs are also applicable to musicians.

An iconic example of a PPR is the defining image on television, and in the newspapers, of Jonny Wilkinson, standing with his hands cupped together as if praying, looking intently back and forth toward the goal during England's triumph in the 2003 Rugby World Cup. This brought world attention to the potential of a PPR in a high-pressure performance situation. Wilkinson's routine helped him focus amidst the tumultuous noise of the crowd, and through hours of practice he had taught himself how to calm his body and mind so that he could produce the perfect goal kick under pressure. Having a routine made him confident that he could achieve this.

Like athletes, musicians have to execute a complicated set of motor skills under a variety of internal and external pressures in order to perform their best. Internal pressures may be felt through physiological symptoms of arousal and/or any number of worrying thoughts. External pressures may come from the performance environment, which could be the audience, the venue and in the case of pianists, the unfamiliar instrument they have to play. Just like Jonny Wilkinson, musicians prior to the performance need to achieve the perfect performance state where they feel confident, motivated, focused, and sufficiently calm; in other words, they have to feel ready to perform.

Research in all performance disciplines, whether sport, the performing arts, surgery, or business, has shown that PPRs can help performers achieve this state of readiness (Cotterill, 2015). Interview studies with professional musicians show that experienced musicians do use routine behaviour to help ready themselves for the performance (Partington, 1995). In my research I wanted to explore how musicians might benefit from the deliberate teaching and development of PPRs as a usual part of their performance preparation.

Summary of the research

During a year-long research project, where I introduced piano teachers to a psychological skills training approach in regular 20- to 30-minute lessons, the relevance and application of PPRs for recreational pianists became evident (Hawkes, 2018). Six female teachers, including me, from a local European Piano Teachers Association professional development group participated in the project. The average number of pupils in each teaching practice was 24. Pupils ranged in age from six years to just over 60 years, and their playing standard ranged from complete beginner to Grade 8.[1] Pupils were all learning the piano as a leisure pursuit.

The research method used was 'Action Research', which is a method that can be used to study the work of practitioners. The aim in my research was to produce both practical (Action) and theoretical (Research) knowledge (McNiff & Whitehead, 2011). I aimed as a practitioner to study my own teaching and as researcher to study the teaching of the other participants. In this Action Research the design comprised two 'cycles of action' during two UK school terms. PPRs were taught to 15 pupils in the first cycle and 21 in the second. In both cycles the teaching began in the four weeks leading up to a performance, which could be an examination or a concert. The aim, five weeks before the performance, was that pupils should have the music well prepared, so the emphasis of the teaching would be on psychological preparation for the performance.

The teaching of PPRs was integrated into regular piano lessons at the teachers' usual place of work; for some at home and for others in school. All the teachers were responsible for choosing the pupils they wished to work with, and how they would implement the routines. At the end of cycle one I conducted a preliminary analysis of the data. This showed that the group were focusing on *how* to teach PPRs rather than *why*. The workshop and meeting that began cycle two addressed this so we could develop our teaching further in the next stage of the research.

At each performance, teachers and pupils evaluated the benefits of PPRs in relation to the performance experience and performance quality. Information about the implementation and the benefits of the PPRs came from pupil and teacher planning sheets, teacher and pupil diaries kept during both action cycles, and from the teacher and pupil performance evaluations written immediately after the performance itself. In the following section both teachers and pupils are referred to by pseudonyms.

Examples of pre-performance routines: more than stage presence

Most PPRs began with a similar suggestion from the teacher:

- Walk up to the piano
- Adjust the stool

- Think
- Bow at the end

This basic routine was developed depending on age, experience, and psychological need. Developmental differences were evident. Younger pupils tended to be teacher-directed as they were not always able to conceptualise or verbalise how they felt about performing. Their routines were typically short and simple. Teacher Lynn, who worked with six young beginners in cycle two, described this very simple routine as a starting point in her teacher diary:

- Walk out and introduce my pieces
- Play
- Bow

The aim was for each pupil to give their 'best possible performance' by learning how to present themselves and 'create a sense of occasion' (Teacher Diary). For some pupils this was their first performance.

Teenage and adult pupils, especially those with more performance experience, were able to verbalise their psychological needs and were more involved in developing and personalising the routines themselves. The teaching approach was mostly pupil directed. An advanced adult pupil of mine, who was an experienced performer, developed a complex routine that started in her seat waiting to perform:

- Breathe in for 5, out for 7, count backwards from 10 to 1
- Walk out
- Adjust stool
- Find pedal
- Positive thinking. Enjoy – tell the story – feel the story – trust yourself
- Visualise the opening bars
- Play – focus on the story
- Bow

(Pupil Diary)

Her aim was also to give her best possible performance, but she knew this could only be achieved if she was relaxed and able to think clearly before and during her performance.

The following vignettes demonstrate how PPRs were implemented in differing performance contexts (cycle one), and how they were further developed for psychological purposes in cycle two. The success of the PPR at the performance as perceived by teacher and pupil is reported.

Vignettes

PPRs for differing performance contexts

Sophie was eight years old and a beginner. She was preparing for a pupil concert and knew her pieces well when the teaching of the PPR began. Teacher Yvonne had noticed she was self-conscious when performing and she thought she could help Sophie overcome this, through getting her to focus on the PPR. This was described in the teacher diary as follows:

- Walk up to piano
- Announce piece
- Music on stand
- Adjust stool
- Check pedal
- Think first phrase
- Count in
- Play
- Wait for applause
- Repeat for second piece
- Bow

Yvonne taught this routine in week one of the four leading up to the concert. In subsequent lessons she checked the learning by asking Sophie to say the routine out loud. The routine was practised in practice performances during each of the four lessons. Sophie also practised the routine at home in mock performances for her grandma and dad. Yvonne wrote that Sophie's performance was 'the best in the concert with a degree of detail which she does not usually show' (Teacher Diary). According to Yvonne, the PPR contributed to this: 'on the day it helped her steady herself and I could see her taking her time and counting in' (Performance Evaluation). Yvonne felt that teaching the PPR had wider influences. Sophie benefited from extra performance practice, which was integral to practising the routine. Yvonne wrote that she 'enjoyed the extra focus and attention'. Sophie herself was too young to analyse the benefits of learning a PPR but she 'enjoyed showing mum and grandma at the same time how good I was' (Pupil Evaluation).

Owen was a teenager preparing for a Grade 5 ABRSM examination. His musical preparation was almost complete four weeks prior to the examination, although Yvonne noted some musical issues he needed to resolve in his pieces, and some aspects of the supporting tests[2] that needed work. Five weeks before the performance Yvonne wrote in her plan that he needed to improve his concentration in both practice and performance, and she hoped that the PPR would help. In his plan the pupil emphasised that more specific practice would improve his confidence. He was clearly worried about mistakes, which would improve if he practised the 'mistake likely section' and if he tried 'to continue after mistakes'. The routine Yvonne developed in lesson one was:

- Walk in
- Adjust stool
- Try out piano
- Think of notes of scale or first phrase
- Wait for the examiner to tell you to begin

In lesson two they had to revise the PPR as Owen had 'forgotten most of it' (Teacher Diary). They also 'established a cut-down version to use to refocus between pieces', the details of which were not recorded. Owen performed the pieces and sight-reading exercise in examination conditions. In lesson three they extended the routine to 'what to think in the waiting room', an idea taken from Gordon (2006). The PPR was then included in a mock examination which was assessed using the exam board's criteria. Lesson four was cut short as Owen was late, which left no time for PPR revision. There was a fifth lesson with a mock examination where Yvonne recapped 'all aspects of the PPR'. There was no evidence from Owen's diary that he practised the PPR regularly at home although he wrote that he needed to practise performing and the PPR as one of his aims for three of the weeks. Owen evaluated that the PPR made him feel 'less nervous in the exam and made me feel like I was ready to play the first note'. Yvonne evaluated that he used the PPR on the day and that his 'confidence levels were high'. He passed the examination.

The integration of specific strategies into PPRs developed for psychological purposes

One strategy used by experienced performers is the use of positive cue words or phrases, spoken or written, either as reminders or as motivators before the performance. Teacher Lynn developed this idea for a student who lacked concentration. She found that several of her young beginners did not concentrate once there was a live audience or when her music room was changed for the concert. She therefore arranged the room as it would be for the concert a few weeks ahead so pupils would get used to the performance environment. Pupils practised the PPR in mock performances in at least three lessons leading up to the concert. Jude, aged six years, found it hard to concentrate on the music when an audience was present. Lynn added stickers on his music to act as performance cues to help him. Jude described his routine in his diary:

- Introduce myself
- Play pieces without stopping
- Look at stickers to remind myself to think about the notes and not the audience
- Take a bow

In her evaluation Lynn thought that introducing himself as well as looking at the stickers helped his concentration. However, she also thought that more performance practice, which was the consequence of practising the PPR, contributed to the 'excellent, confident, fun performance'.

In the next example, deep breathing, a strategy used to help reduce worrying thoughts or feelings, is combined with positive stage behaviour to help the pupil keep calm and confident. Emily, a teenage pupil of mine, lacked confidence when performing. We worked on 'acting confident to feel confident' (see Cuddy, 2012) so she would feel calm enough to focus on the music when she sat down to play. Her routine became:

- Steady breathing
- Walk out with head high
- Adjust stool
- Find hand position
- Think about the start of the piece and dynamics
- Play
- Bow

Emily felt that the PPR helped her to take time so she could think about the piece before playing. She appeared more confident as she walked out and although her routine was a little hurried, she gave a musical and accurate performance. Emily attributed her success to more performance practice in front of family and friends.

In this final example, a well-known relaxation technique is integrated into the PPR.

Angela worked with adult beginner Sarah who told Angela she found it difficult to focus when performing. Angela and Sarah had attended a course on yoga for musicians before the project began (Roskell, n.d.). Angela helped Sarah integrate yoga arm swings at the start of her routine, which she used for her Grade 1 ABRSM examination. Sarah described her PPR as:

- Yoga arm swings
- Walk up to the piano
- Adjust the stool
- Play a scale and broken chord to warm up and try out the piano
- Think before playing

Sarah practised yoga at home regularly as part of her performance routine and also before practising in general as it helped to keep her calm and 'create a proper space for practising the piano' (Pupil Diary) in her busy life. At the examination she thought the yoga helped keep her 'focused and ready to play'. She also wrote, 'Mock examinations with Angela – crucial to managing my expectations and building confidence' (Pupil Evaluation).

Conclusions and implications for practice

PPRs can be developed with pupils at all ages and stages. Developmental differences were evident in the content of the routines. Those developed with younger pupils were teacher directed and simple in content. Routines developed with teenage and adult pupils were pupil directed, longer and more complex. In one sense routines could be considered as learning stage presence, but they were more functional than merely showing a pupil how to walk on and off stage to appear professional to the audience. Similar to the findings in sport, our teaching was not a 'one-size fits all'; the routines for these recreational pianists were individual and seemed to serve the purpose intended by or for that individual (Cotterill, 2011). The basic routine was adapted and appeared to help the pupil achieve better focus or help them maintain a sense of calm and control, which in turn could lead to increased performance confidence.

At the start of the project not all teachers were convinced about the value of teaching psychological skills, or about how adding something else to teach in already busy 20- to 30-minute piano lessons could be beneficial. By the end they acknowledged that PPRs were helpful although three unforeseen consequences of learning and practising PPRs, that may have been contributory factors in the success of the PPRs, were mentioned. Firstly, pupils and teachers noted that practising a PPR led to an increase in practice both of the music and of the performance itself. This increase in practice may have led to increased confidence.

The second consequence was that teaching PPRs improved communication and discussion about performing. The term PPR gave a common terminology which aided communication between teachers, and between teacher and pupil. During the teaching process conversations about performing were opened up that did not exist before. Older pupils were able to talk about strategies that they had developed from other hobbies or instinctively and these could be integrated effectively into their routines. In these conversations younger pupils were given simple reassurances about 'fears of the unknown' in relation to performing. Older pupils were educated about their normal physiological responses to performance pressure.

The final consequence I observed was that through teaching and learning PPRs both teachers and pupils began to conceptualise the difference between learning and practising music and learning and practising the performance. By the end of the project the teachers felt that thinking about and discussing the different types of practice was one of the most helpful aspects of the project. Pupils who conceptualised this difference found it focused their practice in the weeks leading up to the performance.

Research in sport psychology shows that PPRs can be beneficial to elite athletes in a range of sports from basketball to cricket (Cotterill, 2010). Interviews with specialist professional musicians and conservatoire music students show that a variety of routines are used instinctively and are perceived as beneficial as a part of their performance preparation (Hawkes, 2016; Partington, 1995). It is likely that the findings about PPRs in my study are applicable to recreational singers and other instrumentalists when performing solo or in small groups.

The consequence of placing recreational pupils into performance situations for which they are not prepared both musically and psychologically will undoubtedly contribute to poor confidence and may cause some pupils to abandon music lessons altogether. Understanding the benefits of teaching performance strategies, in this case PPRs, shows that more can be done to prepare developing musicians for performance. Furthermore, learning a PPR is useful because it is a transferable skill that pupils can use in other performing activities. Whilst thorough preparation of the music is essential, and inadequate preparation of the music is undoubtedly a factor in undermining performance confidence, this chapter on teaching PPRs shows that performance skills as well as musical ones should be taught from the outset of instrumental learning.

Main points

Pre-performance routines:

- teach stage presence but also serve a psychological purpose
- can be taught at every age and stage of learning
- are developed according to the needs of the individual
- are easy to fit into lessons as part of performance practice

Notes

1 Grades as used by the Associated Board of the Royal Schools of Music (ABRSM) exam system in the UK. Most music exam boards in the UK have eight grade levels, ranging from Grade 1 to Grade 8 (most advanced).
2 Supporting tests in music performance exams assess aural and sight-reading skills. Some exams also include improvisation skills.

References

Cotterill, S. T. (2010). Pre-performance routines in sport: Current understanding and future directions. *International Review of Sport & Exercise Psychology*, *3*(2), 132–154. https://doi.org/10.1080/1750984X.2010.488269

Cotterill, S. T. (2011). Experiences of developing pre-performance routines with elite cricket players. *Journal of Sport Psychology in Action*, *2*(2), 81–91. https://doi.org/10.1080/21520704.2011.584245

Cotterill, S. T. (2015). Preparing for performance: Strategies adopted across performance domains. *The Sport Psychologist*, *29*, 158–170. https://doi.org/10.1123/tsp.2014-0035

Cuddy, A. (2012). *Your body language shapes who you are* [Video]. TED conferences. www.ted.com/talks/amy_cuddy_your_body_language_shapes_who_you_are?

Gordon, S. (2006). *Mastering the art of performance*. Oxford University Press.

Hawkes, M. E. (2016). Enhancing performance: An exploratory study of performance coaching in practice in a UK conservatoire. *Arts and Humanities* in *Higher Education* (Special Issue 2016). www.artsandhumanities.org/journal/ahhe-special-issue-june-2016/

Hawkes, M. E. (2018). *The practical application of psychological skills training for musicians* [Doctoral thesis, The University of Sheffield]. http://etheses.whiterose.ac.uk/24062/

McNiff, J., & Whitehead, J. (2011). *All you need to know about action research.* SAGE.

Moran, A. P. (1996). *The psychology of concentration in sports performers.* Psychology Press.

Moran, A. P. (2004). *Sport and exercise psychology: A critical introduction.* Routledge.

Partington, J. T. (1995). *Making music.* Carleton University Press.

Roskell, P. (n.d.). *Yoga for musicians* [DVD]. www.peneloperoskell.co.uk/yoga/default.html

11 The teacher's role in the enhancement of students' performance experience

Elsa Perdomo-Guevara

Introduction

One of my most painful experiences as a piano teacher was to watch some of my students' shock under the pressure of exams or competitions. This was because I was well acquainted with performance anxiety. It was, in fact, due to performance anxiety that I ended my career as a professional pianist and that I later became involved in psychology and research.

While performance anxiety is prevalent among musicians, there are many performers who love to perform, and we know much less about the factors that might contribute to their experience. Consequently, I focused my research on investigating how these performers thought about performance and how their thoughts differed from performers who do not enjoy performance or who suffer from performance anxiety. In this chapter I discuss the implications that my findings have for teachers.

The link between performers' narratives and performance anxiety

The emotions performers feel during performance are directly linked to the way they think about it; in other words, to the internal conversations that they hold with themselves. While we are seldom aware of it, we continuously create stories in our mind in order to explain to ourselves the meaning of our reality. Research shows that there are some stories that lead to performance anxiety (Kenny, 2011). For instance, when performers tell themselves that a performance is primarily a way for other people to evaluate their work – and, by extension, their value as musicians and human beings – then each performance becomes significant because of the high stakes involved. When, in addition,

DOI: 10.4324/9781003108382-15

they develop an unrealistic mind-set and tell themselves that a performance is only worthwhile if it is perfect and they start viewing even minor errors as catastrophic events, then performance anxiety will be their inevitable companion.

Summary of the research

As I knew first-hand performance anxiety and its characteristic narratives, I was very intrigued by a particular pianist with whom I played when I lived in Brazil. Before going on stage, we were both emotionally activated – I by anxiety and fear, he by excitement and joy. It was evident that our contrasting emotions did not depend on our level of preparation or musical expertise. Therefore, I set out to investigate the kind of stories he and two other friends who loved to perform told themselves about performance. I wondered whether their stories differed from mine and contributed to the joy they drew from performing.

Interviews with these three performers showed quite similar narratives, that differed greatly from the narratives of performers who suffer from anxiety: instead of viewing their audience as critical or hostile, they viewed it as friendly; instead of focusing on what they could receive from the audience (the evaluation), they focused on what they could offer to it; instead of focusing on what they lacked (perfection), they appreciated what they actually had and could share. Instead of telling themselves frightening stories about performance, their stories were inspiring: they viewed performances as opportunities to transcend themselves, contribute, and experience connectedness.

While I was amazed by these results, they concerned only three individuals. Therefore, I decided to conduct a survey to investigate the performance-related narratives of a large number of performers and see whether these were related to their emotions. A total of 625 performers (including professionals, amateurs, and music students) completed my questionnaire.

The findings showed that the narratives of some performers centred on connection and contribution while the narrative of others centred on competence and achievement. Interestingly the former group drew more joy from performance and experienced less anxiety than the latter (Guevara, 2007; Perdomo-Guevara, 2014).

What factors might impact the quality of the performers' narratives? Research shows that the culture to which individuals belong influences their beliefs, values, and goals, and consequently, their narratives (Turner & Stets, 2008). Therefore, I decided to investigate whether there were differences between the narratives of performers who belonged to the classical music milieu, and those of performers who did not. The findings showed that classical music performers were more self-centred and less audience-oriented than non-classical performers; they also enjoyed performance significantly less than their counterparts.

These results suggest that the classical and the non-classical environments implicitly communicate to their members different sets of performance-related beliefs, values, and goals that affect how they come to think and feel about performance. These findings are striking as they challenge the prevalent belief that performance-related emotions are just an individual issue.

The last step of my research aimed at finding out whether performance-related narratives and emotions could be enhanced. To do this, I designed an online course and offered it to any performer who wished to enhance their performance experience. The goal was to help participants develop more inspiring, personally meaningful narratives about themselves, their audience and performance. The course was based on the assumption that best performance experiences would be afforded by narratives that would simultaneously build the performers' sense of relatedness, autonomy, and competence – which are viewed as basic, universal psychological needs (Ryan & Deci, 2000). The course included short videos, practical exercises, and a discussion forum.

The impact of the course was measured through three identical questionnaires that investigated participants' narratives about performance and their emotions during their most recent performance. The first questionnaire was administered just before the course, the second just after the course, and the last one three months afterwards. Seventy participants completed the three questionnaires. The analysis showed that the participants' narratives became more meaningful and self-transcendent after the course and they reported higher performance-related joy, confidence, connection with the audience, sense of contribution, and lower anxiety. The positive impact of the course lasted for at least three months, which suggests that the changes might be long lasting.

Vignettes

Roberto

Roberto was one of the professional musicians whom I interviewed for my first research project. He was a professional harpist playing frequently as a soloist. He drew an incredible joy from performance and had a meaningful, inspiring narrative about it. This is a short excerpt from his interview:

> When you play in public, it is not something mechanical; it is transmission, there is even a spiritual element to it, and all the technical stuff is secondary, I don't even think about it. . . . If there is no transmission . . . there is no point. [. . .] It is like a spiritual transmission, a way of reaching people [. . .] I give myself to the audience. . . . It is the actual offering up of myself that makes me happy.

Clara

Clara was a female horn player, a graduate music student who was applying for a Master's degree. She participated in the online course and left the following comment in the discussion forum after the third week of the course:

> It seems that there is an imaginary line between the auditorium and the stage where there is an abyss that moves us away from the audience. But I think that this abyss is created by social narratives. It is our mission to eliminate this line and show the audience that we are nearer than it seems. I had an audition and I dedicated it to my mother, and this helped me to connect with the audience. This was one of my best auditions. . . . It was the first time that I could connect with the audience and that I was fully inside the music. . . . It was the first time that I didn't care when I missed a note and I continued playing as if nothing had happened. And it was wonderful to have these sensations and to play in such a way. I want to continue working to achieve this at each performance!

Michelle

Michelle was a female pianist and piano teacher. She left this comment some weeks after the end of the course:

> For me, it has always been difficult to play for family, friends, or other people. . . . I felt ashamed. . . . But some weeks ago, I prepared a very special performance for a friend who, unfortunately, was in hospital, waiting for the end of his life. There was an old piano in one of the hospital corridors, available for whoever

wished to play. As I knew my friend loved Zarzuela, I prepared some Zarzuela pieces and there I went. I felt stress and anxiety, but the experience was so gratifying . . . to see how other people were moved by the music. . . . At that moment, my goal, my mission was to give joy to my friend . . . and I learned that things might go better or worse, but I was giving something of myself to another person, something that could take him out of his routine and suffering, and that made me extremely happy. . . . I will always remember his facial expression when he started to cheer up and even started singing the songs that I was playing.

Implications for teachers

The findings of my research showed that even a short online course had a strong influence on the musicians' narratives and, as a result, on the quality of their performance experiences. The course seemed to help participants conceive performance in a way that better fulfilled their psychological needs. For instance, as participants were invited to connect with their personally meaningful reasons for making music, their narratives became more coherent with their sense of self, fulfilling their need for autonomy. As they were helped to increase their appreciation for their skills and strengths, their sense of competence increased as well; as they were made more aware of the performance potential to contribute and afford connectedness, their sense of relatedness with other people involved in the musical experience grew.

Teachers are likely to have a stronger influence on their students' narratives than a short online course. Through the emotional environment teachers create during their lessons, and the values and goals they implicitly communicate, they can help their students build inspiring narratives about themselves, the audience, and performance. As a result, performances are likely to become more meaningful and enjoyable.

When teachers give feedback, the aspects of performance they emphasise make manifest their own approach to performance. Do they view performance as being primarily a means to emotional communication and connection, or as a means to demonstrate expertise? Students assimilate their teacher's values and beliefs automatically, unconsciously, and uncritically, and the teacher's approach to performance is likely to become their own.

When teachers are receptive to the emotions their students intend to communicate through music, when they put their judgemental role on hold, allow themselves to be moved, and respond with empathy to their students' playing, they show that they view music as a communicative language. When in addition they highlight the students' progress and strengths, and their value as musicians and individuals, they make students feel worthy of being listened to. Through their attitude, teachers might help their students develop the mind-set they need to go on stage and enjoy performance.

In contrast, when students only receive negative feedback from their teacher; when they leave the lesson feeling that they are never good enough; when there is never enough time to build the students' appreciation for their own strengths and skills; when there is no room for connection, joy, and celebration during lessons; when perspective is lost and the meaning of music and performance is forgotten, the lesson is likely to become a template for performances deprived of joy and eliciting anxiety.

Music teachers might be viewed as the students' first audience, because they are the ones who first listen to the pieces students play after preparing them at home, and the ones who give them the first performance feedback. Teachers' responses during these regular 'private performances' may shape their students' views of what an audience is like, whether friendly or critical. When teachers are enthusiastic, warm, empathetic and friendly, they increase the likelihood that their students will perceive their audiences in a positive way.

When teachers become aware of the impact they have on their students' self-image, music-related values and beliefs, expectations, achievements, and enjoyment (or lack thereof), they are likely to adopt a broader perspective on their teaching, not only seeking to build their students' musical skills but, most importantly, to help them adopt a positive, inspiring outlook on both themselves and their music-related activities. In order to be successful in these tasks, teachers should acknowledge and meet their students' basic psychological needs.

Teaching in tune with students' psychological needs

While each student is in many ways unique, there are aspects in which all humans are alike. We all need to sleep, drink, and eat to remain alive and physically fit, and in order to experience wellbeing and function at our best, we also need to feel valued, loved by, and connected to other people. We need to feel some measure of control over our lives, and we need to believe that it is within our means to become competent in the activities that matter to us. If any of these needs are neglected, individuals will not experience wellbeing and their performance will suffer (Ryan & Deci, 2000). On the other hand, my research shows that when students are helped to increase their sense of autonomy, competence, and relatedness, their experience is significantly enhanced. It follows from the above that students will benefit greatly if teachers not only seek to enhance their musical expertise but also ensure that their psychological needs are cared for.

Fostering emotional connection

My research findings showed that when participants' sense of connection increased, the joy they drew from performance increased too. Teachers might help their students increase their sense of connection with their audience when, during their lessons, they show their students that they trust and value them. When students feel cared about and emotionally supported by their teachers, they are likely to create a positive mental image of performance and audience. In addition, they might feel safer to explore and expand their horizons, thus, learning at their best, enjoying the process more fully, and developing higher self-confidence (Creech & Hallam, 2011). Therefore, it is important that teachers seek to create an empathetic bond with their students and not merely focus on technical and musical issues during their lessons.

Moreover, teachers should keep in mind that learning a musical instrument is a long-term project that will invariably be marked by periods of doubt, frustration, and discouragement. If they are empathetic and show their students that they are there to help them attain their goals and support them in their challenges, students will feel less lonely and will be more likely to endure during difficult times.

Fostering students' autonomy

My research findings showed that when students' narratives became more personally meaningful – more in tune with their own values and needs – their performance experience became more rewarding too. This suggests that performance-related joy is associated with experiencing a sense of self-expression and authenticity in performance. When performers come to view performance as an opportunity to express their uniqueness, rather than the uniqueness of the composer or their teacher, their need for autonomy is likely to be fulfilled and their experience enhanced. These findings are aligned with research that shows that when students' autonomy is supported, their wellbeing increases (Bonneville-Roussy et al., 2020). In addition, it seems likely that their motivation will increase and that their practice becomes more self-tailored and efficient too.

When teachers strike a balance between structuring their teaching and fostering their students' autonomy, they contribute to their students' wellbeing and best functioning (see also Chapters 4 and 6). In order to do so teachers might, for instance, get interested in and support their students' short- and long-term musical goals; allow them, whenever possible, to choose the pieces they learn, and the way they organise their work; challenge them to solve their technical difficulties, and express their own ideas, images, and feelings regarding the pieces they play.

Fostering students' sense of competence

In order to experience a sense of contribution during performance, performers need to believe that they possess the competences required to perform. For this reason, the online course aimed at increasing the participants' appreciation for their own skills and strengths and aimed at promoting a growth mindset – the belief that through effort and deliberate practice individuals can acquire whatever they need to become competent in what they do. After the course, participants reported that their self-confidence and joy had increased.

When teachers seek to build their students' confidence in their potential and in the positive outcomes associated with hard work and good practice, and do not focus only on correcting errors and improving musical skills, they help their students develop their sense of competence. Students might already be aware of their weaknesses and insufficiencies as musicians and might be victims of the human tendency to amplify what is negative and lose sight of what is positive. They might focus only on what they lack without fully appreciating what they do have. Teachers can help their students develop a more realistic perspective on where they stand on their musical journey by highlighting the progress they have made and the challenges they have overcome. Redirecting students' attention to what they have conquered may give them a more balanced view of themselves and might ensure that they develop the sense of competence that playing before an audience requires.

Conclusion

Teaching in ways that take into account students' psychological needs is a meaningful and challenging endeavour: meaningful, because when teachers appropriately respond to these needs, they help their students to grow in a healthy way, not only as musicians but as human beings too; challenging, because in order to be able to teach in such a human-friendly way, teachers need to look at their own practices with new and critical eyes. Even, most importantly, they need to do hard, introspective work to identify the beliefs and values they express through their practices, evaluate the extent to which these are healthy and inspiring, and, where necessary, work on changing them. This is not an easy task because we all have assumptions about music, our students, and performance that are mostly unconscious. We do not choose our assumptions but, rather, we automatically assimilate them from our social environment – and most likely from our own teachers.

For teachers like me, who belong to the classical music world, our view of students, music, and performance has likely been shaped by what is called 'the conservatoire culture' (Perkins, 2013). This is a culture that values 'talent', achievement, and competition, more than it values emotional connection, psychological wellbeing, self-expression, growth, and fulfilment. Within conservatoire culture, performance and evaluation are inseparable. The values and beliefs that the conservatoire culture promotes (i.e., achievement, perfectionism, competition, the 'talent' of only a few) and those it neglects (i.e., connectedness, autonomy, meaning) do not contribute to individuals' wellbeing but, rather, are likely to foster performance anxiety.

In order to enhance their students' performance experience, teachers might need to become a different type of audience. They might ponder on the extent to which their own stories about teaching and performance are healthy and meaningful, inspiring for their students and inspiring for themselves.

A word of warning is necessary before concluding this chapter. While teachers may do their utmost to help their students enhance their performance experience, it is important to keep in mind that the emotions students experience during performance are shaped by multiple factors (e.g., the student's own personality, level of preparation, their previous experience with performance, their former teachers, or the performance context) and not solely by a teacher's attitude. Therefore, best teaching practices cannot guarantee that students will enjoy performance. They cannot even guarantee that they will not suffer from performance anxiety. Nonetheless, when teachers care for their students' wellbeing; strive to create a teaching environment that simultaneously fosters competence, autonomy, and connection; work on the quality of their own stories about music and performance; and communicate to their students a meaningful and inspiring view of what they do, they are certain to render the teaching-learning experience more rewarding, growth-promoting, and fulfilling for both their students and themselves.

Main points

- There is a link between performers' internal conversations and performance anxiety, which teachers can help to address by cultivating inspiring narratives about performance.
- Some performers focus on connectedness and contribution while others focus on competence and achievement. Asking students about their long- and short-term goals and their challenges will help to reveal these attitudes.
- Musicians who view their audience as friendly and appreciative tend to enjoy performing more. As students' first audience, teachers can help create a positive attitude through their feedback.
- Teachers have a valuable role to play in making students conscious of their strengths, celebrating their performances, and helping them to plan to overcome their challenges and attain their goals.

References

Bonneville-Roussy, A., Hruska, E., & Trower, H. (2020). Teaching music to support students: How autonomy-supportive music teachers increase students' well-being. *Journal of Research in Music Education, 68*(1), 97–119. https://doi.org/10.1177/0022429419897611

Creech, A., & Hallam, S. (2011). Learning a musical instrument: The influence of interpersonal interaction on outcomes for school-aged pupils. *Psychology of Music, 39*(1), 102–122. https://doi.org/10.1177/0305735610370222

Guevara, E. (2007). *Public performance as a joyful, transcendent experience* [Unpublished master's thesis, The University of Sheffield].

Kenny, D. (2011). *The psychology of music performance anxiety.* Oxford University Press.

Perdomo-Guevara, E. (2014). Is music performance anxiety just an individual problem? Exploring the impact of musical environments on performers' approaches to performance and emotions. *Psychomusicology: Music, Mind, and Brain, 24*(1), 66–74. https://doi.org/10.1037/pmu0000028

Perkins, R. (2013). Learning cultures and the conservatoire: An ethnographically-informed case study. *Music Education Research, 15*(2), 196–213. https://doi.org/10.1080/14613808.2012.759551

Ryan, R. M., & Deci, E. L. (2000). Self-determination theory and the facilitation of intrinsic motivation, social development, and well-being. *American Psychologist, 55*(1), 68–78. https://doi.org/10.1037110003–066X.55.1.68

12 Reflections on implications for sound teaching, lifelong music learning, and future research

Henrique Meissner, Renee Timmers, and Stephanie E. Pitts

Connections between findings and applications

Learner-centred approach

Several chapters in this book have demonstrated the importance of a learner-centred approach to vocal and instrumental teaching; tailoring teaching to individual learners and connecting to their experience, ideas, and musical preferences is beneficial for various aspects of musical development. It is important to recognise and respect the various motivations musicians bring to their lessons or group music sessions (Miller; Ayerst) and to be aware of pupils' developmental stages in musical learning (e.g., Hawkes). A learner-centred approach can start with reflection on learning aims and includes consideration of the position of the teachers. Braz Nunes's research has shown how music educators' teaching aims are strongly influenced by their own experiences as students; virtuosic musicians are more likely to focus on high-level performance, while all-round musicians in all probability intend to provide a learner-centred music education. It is important for music educators to be aware of their teaching focus as this can have an effect on their students' confidence and musical development.

Music educators play a role in fostering confidence and enjoyment of performance, whether through empathetic leading of a rehearsal (Bonshor) or the modelling of a focus on connectedness rather than perfection (Perdomo-Guevara). When musical communication takes centre stage in lessons and rehearsals, rather than a 'pedagogy of correction' (Bull, 2021) focusing on 'getting it right' (see also Bull, 2019), this may help with the development of a focus on connectedness in

DOI: 10.4324/9781003108382-16

performance. We acknowledge that this is challenging as communication of musical meaning might need development too, and feedback related to the expression of emotion could also be stressful. It might be difficult to find the right balance, and further research in this area will be required to explore how constructive feedback, containing information about achievements and areas requiring improvement, combined with a focus on empathy and musical communication may support the development of confidence in musicians' performance. In addition, different modes of teaching and feedback (e.g., playing along, turn taking, teaching in groups) may foster confidence, a sense of musical connection as well as enhanced performance (Schiavio et al., 2020).

Musicians' wellbeing was an important theme to music practitioners who attended the *Sound Teaching* (2018, 2019) conferences, particularly topics related to enhancing confidence in performance or dealing with music performance anxiety (see https://mmm.sites.sheffield.ac.uk/for-music-educators). If talking about performance anxiety is a taboo, students may suffer more from this than when it is possible to talk about their fears. It may be useful to explain how anxiety is a very natural response, and talk about the factors that contribute to it, without implying one just has to cope with it. More research is required to develop a cohesive pedagogy on fostering positive attitudes toward music performance, possibly preventing strong forms of anxiety from occurring. Performing is a skill that needs practice, and the research by Hawkes and Perdomo-Guevara has demonstrated that performance strategies can be taught, and positive narratives can be created. Future research may also explore the effects of graded exposure to performing, and performance frequency and experience on young musicians' confidence.

Furthermore, it is important to provide students with opportunities to have autonomy in music learning as this can contribute to wellbeing (Perdomo-Guevara). Providing students and pupils with space for exploration of their own interpretation and pre-performance routines, their understanding of timbre, and methods for learning improvisation skills can all contribute to learners' sense of autonomy. Tutors can provide opportunities for the construction of students' own ideas through dialogic teaching and by modelling various options (Meissner; Ayerst) and being open-minded to novel approaches. The research by both Meissner and Li has shown how tutors' questions can help learners to connect to their embodied experiences of music. Additionally, reflecting on interpretation and timbre, students' development of their own exercises for improvisation or strategies to prepare for performance can facilitate the development of their musical agency, as these activities provide them with opportunities to think of their own musical ideas and their own solutions for music learning problems (cf. Wiggins, 2016). When students' ideas and needs are central in music learning and teaching, musical development can thrive, and musical participation is enhanced.

Music learning through participation and interaction

For many young people and adults, music learning is embedded in musical participation and interaction in groups. Although a learner-centred approach might be easier to implement in individual or small group lessons, it is important to consider this for group music learning too, by adjusting song choice, musical activities, or parts to pupils' interests (Dudson) or level of playing (Miller). In groups with mixed-ability participants, like community music sessions or amateur choir rehearsals, leaders have a role to play in creating a supportive learning environment for all involved. For many musicians, across genres (Miller) and levels of skill (Bonshor), the social aspect of music making, and the enjoyment of musical participation are instrumental for their motivation. Pennill's research shows how the tone for good ensemble interaction is set in first rehearsals, by the ways in which leadership and contributions to rehearsals are distributed, and that it is useful to be aware of the various phases which ensembles may experience over time. It might be interesting to explore these phases in other music learning settings, including interactions between teachers and pupils in one-to-one lessons and the music classroom and how these develop over time.

Music educators learn through participation and interaction too. Braz Nunes recommends that music educators receive professional training that prepares them for the demands of their work (Chapter 2), while Miller mentions that many traditional musicians learn 'on the job' (Chapter 3). These may seem contradictory views (structured and avoiding mistakes vs exploration and trial and error), but both viewpoints are valid and can even be complementary. As pointed out by Braz Nunes, educators should have dedicated professional teaching training because it is important that music teachers are aware of the complexities of their work so that they can be more successful as teachers. It is important that teachers are aware of both the positive and the potentially negative effects of the choices that they make as educators, and the vulnerability of their pupils to having their musical identities shaped and challenged by those choices (MacGregor,

2021). At the same time, Miller's observation is relevant too: educators learn a lot about music teaching by doing and by reflecting on their experiences during the teaching and learning process. It would be valuable to develop communities of music education practice for sharing experiences, for discussing problems and potential solutions, and ideas for pedagogy.

The topics discussed in this book highlight the varied and multifaceted nature of vocal and instrumental music learning and teaching. Musicians are invited to consider the potential applications of these findings in the various settings of their own teaching, rehearsing, or performing practice.

Suggestions for developing research skills as a music practitioner

In all the studies described in this book, practitioner-researchers reflected systematically on their observations, experimental data, and opinions from participants. These systematic observations and reflections helped to construct objective views on the music learning and teaching process. The aim of research is to come to conclusions and implications for practice that are as robust and representative as possible.

Systematic research requires a focus on particular questions and issues, but these can be considered in the context of everyday music practice due to the flexible employment of research methodology (e.g., mixed methods). Reflection combined with a systematic approach to observations can form the starting point for research-informed teaching and performance. Asking questions, testing implicit knowledge, reflecting on teaching or practice strategies, and collecting various views via discussion with colleagues and pupils can be helpful for generating new ideas and enhancing professional practice (cf., Carey et al., 2018; Meissner, 2018).

Because of time-pressures and often isolated working conditions, it is easy to slip into routine teaching or rehearsing strategies over time. As a clarinettist in a previous action research project commented:

> I think when you teach on your own, one to one, (there) is a tendency to just do the same things, the sort of things you've always done. And I really felt it helped . . . to come up with new ideas, or just do things in perhaps a slightly different way, that might help different students in a different way.
>
> (Meissner, 2018, p. 151)

For this clarinettist, participating in a research project had facilitated reflection on teaching practice. Although not everyone has the opportunity to participate in a research project, it may be possible to organise regular informal meetings with like-minded practitioners to discuss ideas and strategies for teaching, performing, or rehearsing. It would be useful if music departments, conservatoires, centres for music education, or music hubs could incorporate occasions for reflection, evaluation, and collaboration into music educators' practice regularly, either by arranging workshops with experienced practitioner-researchers or by providing opportunities for teamwork to discuss methods, share experiences, and acquire new ideas. Music teachers' collaboration is likely to contribute to professional development and improved practice (Carey et al., 2018; Creech & Gaunt, 2018), and such teamwork can be enjoyable and rewarding (Meissner, 2018). Collaboration with colleagues can contribute to the development of a community of practice.

An action research approach could be implemented into musicians' practice to facilitate systematic investigation. Action research consists of various action cycles, each containing the following four steps: (1) practitioners first reflect on potential problems or aspects they want to develop; (2) they make plans to improve practice and implement these plans; (3) they observe the effects of these plans, and (4) they evaluate these effects and make new plans for a new cycle of reflection, action, observation, and evaluation (see Feldman et al., 2018). Keeping a practice diary to document teaching or rehearsing strategies can facilitate reflection on learning and teaching goals, observations, and effects of strategies (Ayerst, see also Hawkes, 2019; Meissner, 2018). Video recordings of rehearsals and lessons and coding of behaviour takes observation a step further. Watching recordings of interactions in lessons or rehearsals can be a formative exercise and has the ability to offer insight into processes that otherwise often remain unaddressed and outside of explicit awareness (e.g., Pennill, 2019).

Implications for lifelong music learning and future research

Learning to play an instrument is widely accepted to be a skill that can be developed throughout the lifespan, perhaps beginning (though not necessarily) with lessons in childhood and opening up opportunities for self-directed playing or group participation for adults at various stages of their lives (see e.g., Pitts, 2020). Learning

Reflections on teaching and learning 137

to teach an instrument can usefully be understood as a similarly lifelong project, needing constant refreshment from new challenges and perspectives.

The research presented in this book and in the much wider available literature on music education and music psychology addresses topics that are of relevance to music educators in a range of contexts: recognising and overcoming performance anxiety, fostering practice strategies and motivation, building a strong foundation for future participation, and creating effective interactions between teachers and pupils. The authors in this book encountered that research through postgraduate studies at the University of Sheffield, and many are now passing on their knowledge through publications, teaching posts, and music leading. Accessing up-to-date research outside a university setting can be more difficult, due to academic publishing models that create paywalls around journal publications, frustratingly limiting the interaction between researchers and practitioners. However, much funded research is now usually available with open access and searching Google Scholar will often lead to a pre-print version of a journal article via a university repository. Other reports are written for a non-academic audience and promoted by organisations including the Incorporated Society of Musicians, Music Mark, and Making Music (e.g., the *State of the Nation* report summarising the alarming decline of music provision in UK schools; All-Party Parliamentary Group for Music Education, 2019). Researchers are increasingly recognising their responsibility to share their work widely, and using podcasts, media, and online platforms to reach audiences outside academia. If all else fails, an email to an author asking for a copy of a recent paper is likely to be well received: researchers generally want to share their work, and to hear from practitioners who are finding their research relevant.

Tools for developing research skills are available through multiple routes, including postgraduate study and accessible methods books written by experienced researchers (e.g. Williamon et al., 2021). Some funding bodies and research centres also provide useful guides to the evaluation of music education and community music projects, such as the toolkits offered by Youth Music (https://network.youthmusic.org.uk/evaluation-guidance-intro) and the Centre for Cultural Value (www.culturehive.co.uk/cultural-value-resources/).

The research reported in this book was conducted before the start of the COVID-19 pandemic. The lockdown periods in 2020 and 2021 accelerated the development of methods and platforms for online learning and performing. Research has already started investigating the effects of remote interaction on music teaching and performing. Several studies have found that musicians miss the embodied experience of musical interaction in physical spaces (e.g., Daffern et al., 2021; Zhu & Pitts, 2021), while some reported the experiences of instrumental tutors who thought that they focused more on student-centred teaching, dialogue, and discussion in online learning environments (De Bruin, 2021). As the enforced online learning of the pandemic settles into new hybrid ways of working, future research will need to explore how communication and music development can best be stimulated in such contexts.

Music teaching and learning is a rich area with still many underexplored questions and issues that warrant further thought and investigation. Dialogue between practice and research is important for research to address the questions that are most in demand, as well as offer insights that can be applied to create positive change. Conferences, organised workshops, and dedicated events hosted by higher education institutions and professional organisations are one way to achieve this – but just as important is the day-to-day engagement with research ideas and with other practitioners.

We would appreciate hearing readers' feedback on the research and its implications presented in this book, as readers' ideas can inform future directions and applications of research. We are aware that this book only addresses a subset of the many processes and issues music teachers engage with on a daily basis. We would be excited to hear how our research can be shaped to have as broad relevance as possible, as well as what essential issues or perspectives it is missing. Collaboration with teachers and performers helps researchers to continue developing and refining research questions and directions. Teaching contexts also offer an essential basis for applied research to be made possible. In this way, research can inform music education and performance practice and vice versa.

References

All-Party Parliamentary Group for Music Education. (2019). *Music education: State of the nation* (Report by the All-Party Parliamentary Group for Music Education, the Incorporated Society of Musicians and the University of Sussex). www.ism.org/images/images/State-of-the-Nation-Music-Education-WEB.pdf

Bull, A. (2019). *Class, control, and classical music.* Oxford University Press.

Bull, A. (2021). Getting it right: Why classical music's "pedagogy of correction" is a barrier to equity. *Music Educators' Journal.*

Carey, G., Coutts, L., Grant, C., Harrison, S., & Dwyer, R. (2018). Music education research enhancing learning and teaching in the tertiary music studio through reflection and collaboration. *Music Education Research, 20*(4), 399–411. https://doi.org/10.1080/14613808.2017.1409204

Creech, A., & Gaunt, H. (2018). The changing face of individual instrumental tuition. In G. E. McPherson & G. F. Welch (Eds.), *Vocal, instrumental, and ensemble learning and teaching. An Oxford handbook of music education, Volume 3* (pp. 145–164). Oxford University Press.

Daffern, H., Balmer, K., & Brereton, J. (2021). Singing together, yet, apart: The experience of UK choir members and facilitators during the Covid-19 pandemic. *Frontiers in Psychology, 12*, 624474. https://doi.org/10.3389/fpsyg.2021.624474

de Bruin, L. R. (2021). Instrumental music educators in a COVID landscape: A reassertion of relationality and connection in teaching practice. *Frontiers in Psychology, 11*, 3995.

Feldman, A., Altrichter, H., Posch, P., & Somekh, B. (2018). *Teachers investigate their work: An introduction to action research across the professions* (3rd ed.). Routledge, Taylor & Francis Group.

Hawkes, M. E. (2019). *The practical application of psychological skills training for musicians* [Doctoral thesis, The University of Sheffield]. http://etheses.whiterose.ac.uk/24062/

MacGregor, E. H. (2021). Conceptualizing musical vulnerability. *Philosophy of Music Education Review.*

Meissner, H. (2018). *Teaching young musicians expressive performance: A mixed methods study* [Doctoral thesis, The University of Sheffield]. http://etheses.whiterose.ac.uk/22929/1/THESIS_HenriqueMeissner.2018.pdf

Pennill, N. (2019). *Working together: Chamber music ensembles in rehearsal* [Doctoral thesis, The University of Sheffield]. https://etheses.whiterose.ac.uk/25132/1/NicolaPennill_PhDthesis_October2019.pdf

Pitts, S. E. (2020). Leisure-time music groups and their localities: Exploring the commercial, educational, and reciprocal relationships of amateur music-making. *Music and Letters, 101*(1), 120–134. https://doi.org/10.1093/ml/gcz044

Schiavio, A., Stupacher, J., Parncutt, R., & Timmers, R. (2020). Learning music from each other: Synchronization, turn-taking, or imitation? *Music Perception, 37*(5), 403–422. https://doi.org/10.1525/mp.2020.37.5.403

Sound teaching. (2018, 2019). Sound Teaching Workshops on Expression, communication and creativity in music performance. www.sheffield.ac.uk/music/research/research-conferences/sound-teaching-workshops-expression-communication-and-creativity-music-performance

Wiggins, J. (2016). Musical agency. In G. E. McPherson (Ed.), *The child as musician: A handbook of musical development* (2nd ed., pp. 102–121). Oxford University Press.

Williamon, A., Ginsborg, J., Perkins, R., & Waddell, G. (2021). *Performing music research: Methods in music education, psychology, and performance science.* Oxford University Press.

Zhu, H., & Pitts, S. E. (2021). When the music stops: The effects of lockdown on amateur music groups. *Journal of Music, Health, and Wellbeing.*

Index

a cappella groups *see* ensembles in rehearsals
accuracy and technique, pursuit of: in classical music 13, 62, 63; in lessons 37, 38, 40, 41, 45, 132–133; and performance anxiety 13, 123, 125, 128, 129, 131; in small ensembles 75, 83; in timbre production 53, 54, 58
aural modelling 31, 38–9, 40–41, 44–45, 52–53, 133; improving accuracy and expressiveness 45; discriminating between different timbres 52; limitations of 44, 53; *see also* expressivity, tools and strategies for teaching; timbre (piano), teaching and learning; traditional music (Scottish)

Bouij, C. 14, 16–17
British Sign Language (BSL) 8, 102, 104–106; *see also* Deaf children, teaching music to; Singing and Signing

choirs: confidence levels in singers, factors affecting 88–89; group dynamics on learning and confidence, effects of 89, 92, 96; group interactions, monitoring of 96; motivations for participating in 92, 134; *see also* ensembles in rehearsals

communication: conductors, styles of 89, 91; in ensembles and groups 75–80, 83, 92, 96, 132, 134; in lessons and teaching 2, 55, 69, 132, 136; of musical character and interpretation 38, 39; of musical meaning 2, 132, 133; musicians and researchers, between 1; in online learning 138; in performance 7, 58; teachers and students, between 107, 119, 130, 137; in timbre production 50, 51, 52; *see also* dialogic teaching
conducting: amateur and formally trained singers, preferences of 90, 92; amateur and professional ensembles 88; musical leadership, as a form of 88, 134; as a pedagogy 87, 88, 92, 94, 95
conductors, verbal feedback from: amateur singers' confidence, influences on 7, 89, 90, 97, 132, 134; amateur singers' interpretations of, factors affecting 91, 92, 96; constructive criticism and detailed praise, positive effects of 92, 93, 95, 97; destructive criticism, negative effects of 91, 94; as experts and role models 90, 95, 97; indiscriminate praise, negative effects of 90, 94; needs of amateur singers, recognising the 91, 95;

task-oriented and person-oriented feedback 95, 97; vague feedback, negative effects of 93, 94
confidence: of amateur singers 7, 88–91, 94; of Deaf pupils 107, 109, 110; in ensembles and groups 81, 92, 96; in improvisation 61; in learning 42; in performance 2, 17, 117, 120, 124, 133; strategies for enhancing 6, 8, 112, 116, 118–119, 128–129; of teachers 17, 18, 20; teachers' influences on students' 95, 96, 97, 132; *see also* enjoyment of music
COVID-19 pandemic 1, 137–138

Dalcroze eurythmics 64, 103
data collection methods: diaries 113–118, 136; drawings and graphic elicitation 65, 78, 107–108; focus groups 25, 88; individual interviews 15, 25, 49, 78, 88, 123; logbook 65; observation 5, 25, 52, 80, 82–83, 136; questionnaire 8, 15, 37, 123–124; video-stimulated recall 38, 42; *see also* research methods
Deaf children, teaching music to: co-leading skills 107, 109; comparisons to hearing children 109–110; dynamic and iterative teaching practices 103; learning and musical preferences of boys 106, 109–110; learning rates for pulse, rhythm, and pitch 109; new musical experiences, exposure to 107; pitch and singing 8, 104–105, 109; pulse and rhythm 8, 103, 107–109; repertoire choice 110; songs and musical games 104–105, 106, 107, 110; speech therapy, musical activities in 108; younger and older children, participation levels of 106; *see also* British Sign Language (BSL); Dalcroze eurhythmics; Kodály approach; Singing and Signing

Deaf and Hearing Impaired (DHI) individuals in music making: musical facility of 104; musical memory of 105; professional music practitioners, lack of 109; professional musicians 101–102, 109; representation, preferences, objections, and misconceptions of 101–102
dialogic teaching 37, 39–42, 133, 137; discussion of musical character 39–43; enhancing interest, enjoyment and motivation in learning 43; exploring musical interpretations 41, 133; questions and dialogue, use of 39, 40, 41, 44; stimulating pupils' thinking and reflection 43, 45; *see also* communication; expressivity, tools and strategies for teaching

embodied music cognition and learning 3, 133
engagement in music: of Deaf students 102, 103, 106–107, 110; early years, during 15; enabling 8, 37, 103; improvisation, in learning 70; listening as type of 31; promoting students' 18, 22; social engagement, in the context of 28; teachers' influences on students' 21, 69; *see also* participation in music
enjoyment of music 2; in Deaf students 107, 108; in ensembles and groups 7, 28, 91, 93, 134; performance, during 111, 122, 124, 126, 131; strategies for enhancing 6, 8, 43, 45, 95, 96; in teaching and learning 18–19, 20, 22, 114–115, 127–128, 131–132; *see also* confidence
ensembles in rehearsals: characteristics of small groups 75–76; communication and development, dynamic and non-linear progress in 83; exploration,

transition, and integration, developmental phases of 78–79; first meeting, reality check, and shared achievement, key events of 80–82; first rehearsal, dynamics of the 82–83, 134; interaction patterns, evolving changes in 79; new and established ensembles, differences between 77; rapid transitions between developmental phases 78, 84; rehearsals, effective planning of 84–85, 134; theories of team development, parallels to 83, 85; types of verbal and non-verbal communication 7, 77; verbal to non-verbal communication, shifting from 79, 85; *see also* choirs

establishing agency as a learner 134; in improvisation 68, 71; in Scottish traditional music 25; in small ensembles 76

expressivity: and limitations of music notation 38; and performance anxiety 44, 45, 137; as a talent and a learned skill 37, 43; in young children 43, 45

expressivity, tools and strategies for teaching: articulation, dynamics, tempo, timbre, timing, and ornamentation 38; aural modelling, metaphors, gestures, imagery, and movement 38, 39, 40, 41, 44; combining strategies for different learning stages 6–7, 41–45; focusing on character over technique and note-reading 41; limitations of certain strategies 39; openness to pupils' interpretations 43, 45; s*ee also* dialogic teaching

Fux, J. 64, 69

Goehr, L. 63
group leadership *see* teachers as leaders and role models

improvisation (classical music): emotional and cognitive barriers to learning 61, 62, 63; freedom, control, and stylistic constraints in 64, 67; general pedagogic strategies, challenges of 68–69; lack of training in 7, 61, 68; non-improvising musical culture, influences of a 62, 70

improvisational *knowledge*, learning and acquisition of: basic vocabulary, stylistic understanding, and underlying rules 64; conscious to intuitive improvising, shifting from 68; conversion of existing musical knowledge 66; fixed musical views to musical possibilities, moving from 67–68; skills in attention, decision-making, and analysis 66; theoretical, embodied, and agentic knowledge, types of 70; underlying musical concepts, structures, and principles 67; *see also* improvisation skills, *mobilising*

improvisation skills, *mobilising*: developing an improvisatory *disposition* 63; flexible and individual learning approaches 69–71; inventing exercises and learning strategies 7, 68, 70, 71; learning processes over musical results, focusing on 65, 68; practical experience, gaining of 70–71; reflecting, drawing, and writing about the learning process 65; rules as guidelines, usage of 69; *see also* improvisational *knowledge*, learning and acquisition of

institutional expectations on students and educators 13
interaction *see* communication

Jaques-Dalcroze, E. 64 *see also* Dalcroze eurhythmics

144 Index

Kodály approach 103 *see also* Dalcroze eurhythmics

learner-centred teaching approach 118, 132; *see also* needs of music learners
learning experiences *see* teachers' attitudes towards music education

motivation: different types of student 28, 31, 92, 132, 134; in ensembles and groups 81; improvisation, in teaching and learning 69, 71; performance preparation, during 112, 117; promoting and enhancing students' 18, 43, 128, 137; in Scottish traditional music 28, 31; teachers' influences on students' 90; in teaching and learning 45
music psychology research, processes and applications 3, 8

needs of music learners: as adult amateur singers 91, 92; as Deaf young people 108; as student performers 114, 120, 124, 126–129; teachers addressing the 3, 19, 20, 22, 134; *see also* learner-centred teaching approach; performers' psychological needs, teachers addressing

online teaching and performing, research into 138

participation in music 2; of Deaf children 8, 101, 102, 105–108; ensembles and groups, within 85, 88, 92; of performers and listeners 6; in Scottish traditional music 6, 25–28, 30–32; teaching and learning, during 45, 52, 134; *see also* engagement in music
performance anxiety 2, 3; conservatoire culture, in the 130, 137; internal and external pressures 112, 127; performance strategies, future research into 133; performers' narratives and, links between 2, 122–123, 131; preparation of music 120; preparing pupils, lack of guidance in 111; strategies for coping with 124, 126, 133, 137; students' performing experiences, factors affecting 44–45, 130
performance narratives: classical and non-classical musicians', differences between 124; on connectedness, contribution, competence, and achievement 123, 126, 131, 132; for enhancing performance experience 124–126; performer, the audience, and the performance, on the 122–124; of performers who enjoy performing 123, 125, 131; of performers who experience anxiety 123; teachers' influences on cultivating meaningful 126–127, 131, 132, 134; *see also* performers' psychological needs, teachers addressing
performers' psychological needs, teachers addressing: autonomy and self-expression, fostering 128, 133; competence and confidence, fostering a sense of 8, 129, 132–133; emotional connection and empathy, fostering 128, 132; teaching narratives, improving the quality of 129–130; *see also* learner-centred teaching approach; needs of music learners; performance narratives
pre-performance routines (PPR): of athletes 111–112, 119; improving music performing experiences with 8, 115–119; in sport psychology 111; state of readiness through, achieving a 112; as a transferable skill 120; *see also* Wilkinson, J.

pre-performance routines (PPR) in different musical contexts: advanced adult students, pre-concert routine for 114; beginner adult students, pre-exam routine for 118; beginner younger pupils, pre-concert routine for 115; concentration and anxiety, integration of strategies for 116–118; at every age and stage of learning 120; individual routines and developmental differences 118, 120; revision of 116; teacher-directed and pupil-directed routines 114, 118; teaching stage presence using 118, 120; teenage intermediate students, pre-exam routine for 116; teenage students, pre-concert routine for 117

Portuguese philharmonic bands (bandas filarmónicas) 13, 15, 19, 21, 22

research methods: action research 5, 37, 39–41, 113, 135, 136; autoethnography 5, 61, 65, 69; ethnography 5, 25, 31; experimental study 5, 39, 40, 42, 51; exploratory study 5, 8, 103; Interpretative Phenomenological Analysis (IPA) 88–9; longitudinal case study 7, 77; mixed methods approach 5, 7, 38, 135; qualitative study 25, 37, 88–89; systematic research and reflection 1, 135, 136; thematic analysis 77; see also data collection methods

Rosen, C. 51–52

Singing and Signing 8, 102, 108, 110; see also British Sign Language (BSL); Deaf children, teaching music to

Sound Teaching Conference, Sheffield 2, 133

teachers' attitudes towards music education 16–22, 132; early, mid, and late career stages, influences of 15, 16, 19, 20, 21, 22; negative musical memories, influences of 16, 17, 18, 132; positive musical memories, influences of 17, 22, 132; teaching contexts, influences of 18–19

teacher demonstrations see aural modelling

teachers' educational and professional journeys 15

teachers as leaders and role models 6, 134; conductors 88, 95; Deaf and hearing music leaders 103, 105, 109; Deaf professional musicians 102, 109; late-career teachers 20; in Scottish traditional music 28, 30

teachers' past experiences as students 14, 16, 22, 132

teachers and researchers, ways of connecting 1, 136, 137, 138; research skills for musicians, tools and sources for 137

teacher training support, lack of 20, 21, 22, 134

teaching and learning: different modes of 31, 133; as lifelong skills 136–137; multifaceted nature of 135; as a reflective practice 22, 132, 134, 135; routine teaching and rehearsing 135

timbre (piano): acoustical perspectives of 50; as an embodied and blended concept 49, 55, 133; expanding notions beyond sonic dimensions 57; as a holistic and cross-modal experience 49, 52; as a lifelong skill and learning process 53, 55; limitations in the variations of 48; multiple levels of body-mind integration 57, 58; pianists' conceptions of 49–50; visual-based (movement and gestures) perceptions of 50–51, 55–56

timbre (piano), teaching and learning: aural sensitivity, cultivation of 48, 57, 58; bodily sensations, proprioceptive, and interoceptive feelings 52, 55, 57–58; gestures as visual communication during performance, use of 58; hand shapes and performative gestures, use of 55–56; low-quality instruments, consequences of 57; questions, dialogue, and instructive language, use of 55, 57, 133; student-teacher co-constructions of timbral concepts 52, 56, 133; touch qualities, energy, force, weight, tension, and relaxation, use of 54; in young children and early stages of learning 53, 58; *see also* aural modelling; dialogic teaching

traditional music (Scottish) 3, 4, 6, 24–32, 134; formulaic variation in 'Spootiskerry' 28–29; Glasgow Fiddle Workshop (GFW) 25–32; listening as participation 28, 137; mixed approaches of learning strategies 26, 27, 30, 31; mixed expertise community and ability groups 26, 30, 134; oral-aural learning 25–26; participation and contribution, value of 27–28, 30, 32, 134, 137; self-regulation of musical participation 26; slow sessions and participatory performance 25, 27–30, 137; social and inclusive musical genre 24–25, 27–29, 30, 31, 134; transmission of 24

wellbeing of musicians 127–130, 133

Werktreue 63

Wilkinson, J. 112 *see also* pre-performance routines (PPR)

For Product Safety Concerns and Information please contact our EU representative GPSR@taylorandfrancis.com
Taylor & Francis Verlag GmbH, Kaufingerstraße 24, 80331 München, Germany

www.ingramcontent.com/pod-product-compliance
Lightning Source LLC
Chambersburg PA
CBHW051749230426
43670CB00012B/2213